THE HAMLYN L]
FIFTY-FIRST SERIES

THE STATE OF JUSTICE

AUSTRALIA
LBC Information Services—Sydney

CANADA and USA
Carswell—Toronto

NEW ZEALAND
Brooker's—Auckland

SINGAPORE and MALAYSIA
Sweet & Maxwell Asia—Singapore and Kuala Lumpur

THE STATE OF JUSTICE

by

MICHAEL ZANDER Q.C.
Emeritus Professor, London School of Economics

Published under the auspices of
THE HAMLYN TRUST

LONDON
SWEET & MAXWELL
2000

*Published in 2000 by Sweet & Maxwell Limited of
100 Avenue Road, Swiss Cottage,
London NW3 3PF
Typeset by LBJ Typesetting Ltd of Kingsclere
Printed in England by
MPG Books Ltd, Bodmin, Cornwall*

No natural forests were destroyed to make this product;
only farmed timber was used and replanted

A CIP catalogue record for this book is available from the British
Library

ISBN 0 421 729708 (HB)
0 421 729805 (PB)

All rights reserved. U.K. statutory material in this publication
is acknowledged as Crown copyright.
No part of this publication may be reproduced or transmitted
in any form or by any means, or stored in any retrieval system
of any nature without prior written permission,
except for permitted fair dealing under the Copyright, Designs and
Patents Act 1988,
or in accordance with the terms of a licence issued by the
Copyright Licensing Agency in respect of photocopying and/or
reprographic reproduction. Application for
permission for other use of copyright material
including permission to reproduce extracts in other
published works shall be made
to the publishers. Full acknowledgment of author, publisher
and source must be given.

©
Michael Zander Q.C.
2000

TABLE OF CONTENTS

Contents   v
The Hamlyn Lectures   vii
The Hamlyn Trust   xi

1. JUSTICE AND ACCESS TO JUSTICE   1
2. CIVIL JUSTICE   27
3. CRIMINAL JUSTICE   51
4. HUMAN RIGHTS   77

Index   105

THE HAMLYN LECTURES

1949 Freedom under the Law
    by the Rt Hon. Lord Denning

1950 The Inheritance of the Common Law
    by Richard O'Sullivan, Esq.

1951 The Rational Strength of English Law
    by Professor F.H. Lawson

1952 English Law and the Moral Law
    by Professor A.L. Goodhart

1953 The Queen's Peace
    by Sir Carleton Kemp Allen

1954 Executive Discretion and Judicial Control
    by Professor C.J. Hamson

1955 The Proof of Guilt
    by Professor Glanville Williams

1956 Trial by Jury
    by the Rt Hon. Lord Devlin

1957 Protection from Power under English Law
    by the Rt Hon. Lord MacDermott

1958 The Sanctity of Contracts in English Law
    by Professor Sir David Hughes Parry

1959 Judge and Jurist in the Reign of Victoria
    by C.H.S. Fifoot, Esq.

The Hamlyn Lectures

1960　The Common Law in India
　　　by M.C. Setalvad, Esq.

1961　British Justice: The Scottish Contribution
　　　by Professor Sir Thomas Smith

1962　Lawyer and Litigant in England
　　　by the Rt Hon. Sir Robert Megarry

1963　Crime and the Criminal Law
　　　by the Baroness Wootton of Abinger

1964　Law and Lawyers in the United States
　　　by Dean Erwin N. Griswold

1965　New Law for a New World?
　　　by the Rt Hon. Lord Tanley

1966　Other People's Law
　　　by the Rt Hon. Lord Kilbrandon

1967　The Contribution of English Law to South African Law: and the Rule of Law in South Africa
　　　by the Hon. O.D. Schreiner

1968　Justice in the Welfare State
　　　by Professor H. Street

1969　The British Tradition in Canadian Law
　　　by the Hon. Bora Laskin

1970　The English Judge
　　　by Henry Cecil

1971　Punishment, Prison and the Public
　　　by Professor Sir Rupert Cross

1972　Labour and the Law
　　　by Professor Sir Otto Kahn-Freund

1973　Maladministration and its Remedies
　　　by Sir Kenneth Wheare

The Hamlyn Lectures

1974 English Law—the New Dimension
   by the Rt Hon. Lord Scarman

1975 The Land and the Development; or, The Turmoil and the Torment
   by Sir Desmond Heap

1976 The National Insurance Commissioners
   by Sir Robert Micklethwait

1977 The European Communities and the Rule of Law
   by Lord Mackenzie Stuart

1978 Liberty, Law and Justice
   by Professor Sir Norman Anderson

1979 Social History and Law Reform
   by Professor Lord McGregor of Durris

1980 Constitutional Fundamentals
   by Professor Sir William Wade

1981 Intolerable Inquisition? Reflections on the Law of Tax
   by Hubert Monroe

1982 The Quest for Security: Employees, Tenants, Wives
   by Professor Tony Honoré

1983 Hamlyn Revisited: The British Legal System Today
   by Lord Hailsham of St Marylebone

1984 The Development of Consumer Law and Policy—Bold Spirits and Timorous Souls
   by Sir Gordon Borrie

1985 Law and Order
   by Professor Ralf Dahrendorf

1986 The Fabric of English Civil Justice
   by Sir Jack Jacob

The Hamlyn Lectures

1987 Pragmatism and Theory in English Law
    by P.S. Atiyah

1988 Justification and Excuse in the Criminal Law
    by J.C. Smith

1989 Protection of the Public—A New Challenge
    by the Rt Hon. Lord Justice Woolf

1990 The United Kingdom and Human Rights
    by Dr Claire Palley

1991 Introducing a European Legal Order
    by Gordon Slynn

1992 Speech & Respect
    by Professor Richard Abel

1993 The Administration of Justice
    by Lord Mackay of Clashfern

1994 Blackstone's Tower: The English Law School
    by Professor William Twining

1995 From the Test Tube to the Coffin: Choice and Regulation in Private Life
    by the Hon. Mrs Justice Hale

1996 Turning Points of the Common law
    by the Rt Hon. The Lord Cooke of Thorndon KBE

1997 Commercial Law in the Next Millennium
    by Professor Roy Goode

1998 Freedom Law and Justice
    by the Rt Hon. Lord Justice Sedley

1999 The State of Justice
    by Michael Zander Q.C.

THE HAMLYN TRUST

The Hamlyn Trust owes its existence to the will of the late Miss Emma Warburton Hamlyn of Torquay, who died in 1941 at the age of 80. She came of an old and well-known Devon family. Her father, William Bussell Hamlyn, practised in Torquay as a solicitor and J.P. for many years, and it seems likely that Miss Hamlyn founded the trust in his memory. Emma Hamlyn was a woman of strong character, intelligent and cultured, well-versed in literature, music and art, and a lover of her country. She travelled extensively in Europe and Egypt, and apparently took considerable interest in the law and ethnology of the countries and cultures that she visited. An account of Miss Hamlyn by Dr Chantal Stebbings of the University of Exeter may be found, under the title "The Hamlyn Legacy", in volume 42 of the published lectures.

Miss Hamlyn bequeathed the residue of her estate on trust in terms which it seems were her own. The wording was thought to be vague, and the will was taken to the Chancery Division of the High Court, which in November 1948 approved a Scheme for the administration of the trust. Paragraph 3 of the Scheme, which closely follows Miss Hamlyn's own wording, is as follows:

> "The object of the charity is the furtherance by lectures or otherwise among the Common People of the United Kingdom of Great Britain and Northern Ireland of the knowledge of the Comparative Jurisprudence and Ethnology of the Chief European countries including the United Kingdom, and the circumstances of the growth of such jurisprudence to the Intent that the Common People of the United Kingdom may realise the privileges which in law and custom they enjoy in comparison with other European Peoples and realising and appreciating such privileges may recognise the responsibilities and obligations attaching to them."

The Hamlyn Trust

The Trustees are to include the Vice-Chancellor of the University of Exeter, representatives of the Universities of London, Leeds, Glasgow, Belfast and Wales and persons co-opted. At present there are nine Trustees:

Professor J.A. Andrews, C.B.E., M.A., BCL
Professor J.W. Bridge, LL.B., LL.M., Ph.D [representing the Vice-Chancellor of the University of Exeter] (Chairman)
Professor N. Dawson, LL.B.
Professor D.S. Greer, Q.C. (Hon.), LL.D., BCL
Professor B.A.K. Rider, LL.B., LL.M., Ph.D
Mr P.J. Seago, O.B.E., J.P., LL.M.
Professor A.J. Ogus, M.A., BCL
The Rt Hon. The Lord Justice Sedley
Professor J.M. Thomson, LL.B.

From the outset it was decided that the objects of the Trust could best be achieved by means of an annual course of public lectures of outstanding interest and quality by eminent Lecturers, and by their subsequent publication and distribution to a wider audience. The first of these Lectures were delivered by the Rt Hon. Lord Justice Denning (as he then was) in 1949. Since then there has been an unbroken series of annual Lectures. A complete list of the Lectures may be found on pages vii to x. The Trustees have also, from time to time, provided financial support for a variety of projects which, in various ways, have disseminated knowledge or have promoted a wider public understanding of the law. One such project, undertaken by the Centre for Criminal Justice Studies of the University of Leeds, has produced the website "U.K. Law Online: The U.K. Legal System on the Internet": see http://www.leeds.ac.uk/law/hamlyn/.

This, the 51st series of Lectures, was delivered by Professor Michael Zander at the London School of Economics and Political Science in November and December 1999.

January 2000 **JOHN BRIDGE**
Chairman of the Trustees

1. Justice and Access to Justice

It is a great honour to be invited to give the Hamlyn Lectures. The roll of former lecturers in this series (including such names as Denning, Devlin, Kahn-Freund, Glanville Williams and Scarman) is a glittering array. To be asked to join such an illustrious company is not only an honour, it is also a formidable challenge. The fact that these lectures, the 51st in the series, are given in the last days of the twentieth century is also pregnant with overtones. I hope that the title for the series—*The State of Justice*—has about it the appropriate aura of significance for so portentous a moment in time.

I am delighted that it has been possible to arrange for all four lectures to be given here at the London School of Economics and I thank the School and the Law Department for this courtesy. I am also most honoured that this lecture should be chaired by Lord Browne-Wilkinson, the senior law lord.

The subject embraced by the title for the series "The State of Justice" is so vast that four lectures can do no more than scratch the surface. However broad the brush one cannot even touch on, let alone treat, every relevant topic. My aim in each lecture has been to focus on as many as possible of the most important issues. But I am very conscious that for reasons of space or for lack of competence (or both) there are major issues that I do not address at all. (In this lecture, for instance, I say nothing on the important issue of quality of legal services; in my lecture on criminal justice I say nothing about the race question or victims or the penal system.)

There are those who believe that the British justice system is the best in the world—and for all I know it may be. But I have always resisted the temptation to make such a global statement about our system in comparison with others because I find it impossible to evaluate our system as a whole much less everyone else's. A legal system has an infinite number of working parts. To get a sense of a national system one has to put as many as possible of those working parts under scrutiny. The right answer to the question whether the legal system in a particular country at a particular time is good or not so good is therefore to ask the question "in what respect?". It is through the aggregate of detailed evaluations of the different parts of the system that one may eventually arrive at an overall conclusion. But for me the overall conclusion is far less interesting than the detailed evaluations. For one person may emphasise the observed warts, where someone else, who has seen exactly the same blemishes, may emphasise other more benign features. One sees the glass half empty, another sees the same glass half full. I would acknowledge that my own tendency over the years has been to focus more attention on the weak features, rather than on the strong features.

By what criteria can one judge a legal system? My title suggests that one criterion is the quantity and quality of justice that it delivers, and if that could be ascertained it would surely be the most important criterion of all. But I am not sure that the question can be put meaningfully, let alone answered. The trouble is that we do not have any means for measuring the justice quotient in decisions of the courts. Take criminal cases. When a person is found guilty we do not normally know whether he actually is guilty. Even when he pleads guilty we cannot be sure that he committed the act in question. He might be completely innocent. When someone is acquitted the press often refer to him as "found innocent" but that is plainly wrong. Acquitted means only what it says—found not guilty—which might also be rendered not found guilty. How can one measure whether the verdict was just? Sometimes one does have a distinct sense that justice has been done in an individual case, though it also happens that that firm impression is sometimes later shown to have been mistaken. But I know of no way of assessing to what extent "justice" was done in a sample of cases whether civil or criminal. The question is too elusive, too complex to unravel. It would require knowledge of too many unknowable facts. The concept of justice in legal cases I suspect is too deep for any research project. At all events, so far as I am aware it has not been attempted. We cannot therefore reach a view as to the proportion of cases in which courts reach a "just" result.

One can ask the less demanding question whether the result was understandable in terms of the evidence, and attempts of that kind have been made. But even then, whose view is then being represented? The researcher could only form his own view if he was able to follow the whole case from start to finish, preferably including all its pre-trial stages. To do that for one case is difficult enough. To do it for even a small number of cases is in practice almost impossible. To do it for a large sample is probably impossible.

One can ask the participants in the case for their view and that has been done. It provides an answer of sorts but if one asks different participants one gets different impressions. Then where is the truth of the matter? I learnt the lesson in the Crown Court Study which I conducted for the Runciman Royal Commission on Criminal Justice.[1] We asked the different participants in a large sample of Crown Court cases to fill out questionnaires as soon as the case was concluded. It was remarkable how often they disagreed as to what happened at the trial even on simple questions of fact.

If measuring what I am calling the justice quotient in the system is impossible, it is equally vain to imagine that one can assess the injustice quotient. The Runciman Commission was established because even Mrs Thatcher, who despised Royal Commissions, had been persuaded that one was needed to deal with mounting public anxiety about miscarriage of justice cases involving prosecution misconduct.[2] This public anxiety had been generated by a handful of major cases all, as bad luck would have it, involving IRA terrorism.[3] The fact that concerns serious enough to cause the setting up of a Royal Commission were provoked by a tiny number of high profile cases, said more about political sensitivity than it did about the scale of the problem of miscarriages of justice. The Royal Commission considered trying to estimate how many persons in prison might be victims of a miscarriage of justice, but decided that there was no way in which such an estimate could be based on anything solid. The number of such cases and therefore their statistical frequency will always be unknowable.

---

[1] The writer was also a member of the Royal Commission.
[2] The establishment of the Royal Commission was in fact announced shortly after her successor Mr John Major became Prime Minister.
[3] Principally the cases of "the Guildford Four", the Maguires and "the Birmingham Six". The setting up of the Royal Commission was announced on the day that the Court of Appeal quashed the convictions of "the Birmingham Six".

One might say that evidence that *any* such cases occur is sufficient. Since a legal system should not perpetuate miscarriages of justice, the fact that some occur is evidence that the system is failing. But this approach cannot be regarded as serious. No system can avoid making some mistakes. Even if the system were perfectly designed there would always be the possibility of miscarriages of justice caused by human error, in the form, for instance, of mistaken eyewitnesses or human wickedness, say, of lying witnesses.

Also, what could be said to be a "mistake" may be a better reflection of justice than a "true verdict" based on the law and the evidence. When the jury acquitted Clive Ponting (1985)[4] or Pat Pottle and Michael Randall (1991)[5] some would say that the result was "right" meaning "just", even though the jury in both cases was plainly defying both the law and the evidence.

Nor can the quotient of justice delivered by the system be measured sensibly by its outcomes. There is no "right" percentage of acquittals in criminal cases or of verdicts for the claimant in civil cases. Each national system will have its recognisable typical current profile which tends to be pretty consistent year on year. These national profiles vary from country to country but again the variations tell us nothing about the justice factor. So the fact that the English criminal justice system has a much higher proportion of acquittals than another could reflect different levels of "justice" obtainable in the two systems. However, it may just reflect different systems of pre-trial screening. Weak cases that in our system end with an acquittal may in the other system be weeded out at an earlier stage by a more rigorous system of pre-trial scrutiny. Similarly the fact that in our system juries acquit more often than magistrates does not establish that juries do more justice. We have no sound basis for judging that juries are right and magistrates wrong.

Leaving aside the question of evaluating the "justice quotient", if one asks then by what criteria should one attempt to evaluate a legal system, there are many that are relevant. In the case of civil justice, for instance, the issues include: how

---

[4] Ponting, a senior civil servant, was prosecuted under the Official Secrets Act for leaking information to an MP about the sinking of the Argentinian ship *The General Belgrano* during the Falklands War.

[5] Pottle and Randall were prosecuted for helping the spy George Blake to escape from prison 25 years earlier. They were prosecuted after they wrote a book about their exploit.

accessible is the system in terms of cost, simplicity of procedure and the geographical availability of courts; how bad are the delays; are there appropriate sticks and carrots to encourage out of court settlements; are there alternative dispute resolution systems; are judges and cases matched appropriately; does the system for the listing of cases work with reasonable efficiency from the perspective both of the professionals and of witnesses; is the system for enforcing judgment debts efficient? There are equivalent questions with regard to criminal cases. In both civil and criminal cases the fundamental question is whether the system holds the balance fairly between the parties, though the nature of the desired balance is somewhat different. In civil cases, the aim is that so far as practicable one should try to have a level playing field between the two sides. In criminal cases it is accepted that fairness includes the principle that the playing field should be somewhat tipped in favour of the defence, for instance in regard to the burden of proof or pre-trial disclosure. Also, the appropriate balance between the two sides has to be weighed in the light of the need for due economy and efficiency. So in regard to criminal justice, on some topics primary weight is given to the interests of the prosecution (sometimes called the "crime control" perspective), and on others to the interests of the suspect (sometimes called the "due process" perspective), and on others again to the need for economy and efficiency.

Inevitably, everyone brings to the task his or her own perspective. A civil libertarian strikes the balance differently from a police officer. It was difficult, for instance, to find amongst the 600 or more submissions of evidence to the Runciman Royal Commission any that were themselves balanced—in the sense of weighing pros and cons. Almost always they set forth views and recommendations with no acknowledgment that there could be plausible contrary opinions. Yet on most important questions there are plausible alternative views.

One hopes that the way is lighted by relevant empirical evidence whether in the form of data collected on a regular basis, such as the annual *Criminal Statistics* or *Judicial Statistics*, or in the form of ad hoc studies. By comparison with many countries we are relatively fortunate in the amount of information about the operation of the system that is available, and over the past 20 years there has been a considerable increase in the amount of empirical research that is undertaken. Even the Lord

Chancellor's Department, formerly laggard in undertaking or commissioning research, now commits funds on a worthwhile scale to this enterprise. Yet, despite the undoubted improvement of recent years, it is remarkable how often one comes across a question on which there is either no information or wholly inadequate information. It is even more remarkable how often Government makes policy decisions in a state of ignorance of important relevant facts.

Whether one's view of these issues can helpfully be informed by formal guiding principles is a matter of opinion. The Runciman Commission's Report was criticised by some commentators for its failure to use the principles embedded in the European Convention on Human Rights as one of its lodestars.[6] I was not persuaded by this criticism. In my view, whether operating on one's own or in a committee with others, one brings to the question one's own values, knowledge and experience. General principles, however relevant and weighty, will only be brought to bear to the extent that they are felt to be applicable to the particular question. That cannot be determined by the general principle. It is determined rather by how the individual feels about that problem in light of his knowledge and experience. So the civil libertarian may, on a particular topic, adopt the police officer's "crime control" approach to the problem, and vice versa. In each case it is not the general principle that produces the result but the person's sense that on that topic that is the right approach.

These four lectures on the State of Justice at the end of the millennium reflect the views of an academic lawyer who for many years has been a student of the workings of the legal system and in particular of the system's pathology.

* * *

The phrase "Access to Justice" has become a term of art signifying the arrangements made by the state to ensure that the public at large and especially those who are indigent can obtain the benefits available through the use of law and the legal system. This country has been a leader in addressing that problem. In particular, we have had a legal aid system that is

---

[6] See for instance A. Ashworth, *The Criminal Process*, (1994, Clarendon, Oxford), pp. 292–296.

remarkable both for its scope and for the fact that it involves so large a proportion of the legal profession. It was established as one of the great reforms introduced by the post-War Atlee Government. The Legal Aid Act 1949 setting up the civil legal aid scheme was a historic stage in the story of legal services for the poor. Over the past five decades there have been many important developments in the legal aid scheme, but, after 1949, unquestionably the next most important milestone is 1999, (exactly 50 years later) and the Access to Justice Act of this year, though the new Act is a milestone of a very different kind. The 1949 Act was an opening of the door to justice for citizens. The 1999 Act has in effect erected a large notice over that door entitled "Restricted Entry". The significance of that change is the main focus of this lecture.

The essence of the system established by the 1949 Act was that if a citizen with a legal problem could establish that he or she qualified for legal aid under the means test and the merits test, he or she had an *entitlement* to legal aid. There was an annual budget approved by Parliament, but if the budget was exceeded a supplementary grant was always obtained. The same concept applied to legal aid for criminal cases. If the court was satisfied that the defendant qualified under the means test and the merits test it granted legal aid and again the taxpayer would foot the bill. In 1998 the total bill was roughly £1.6 billion net—not a small sum.

From the 1980s onward the rising cost to the taxpayer of the legal aid budget increasingly became a matter of political concern. Rightly or wrongly (this is not the occasion for discussion of that issue) the previous Lord Chancellor, Lord Mackay, responded to pressure from the Treasury in a Green Paper in July 1995[7] in which he outlined radical proposals for altering the existing legal aid scheme. Of the many proposals in that Green Paper, by far the most important was that legal aid expenditure, instead of being demand-led and open-ended, should be capped or subject to a ceiling. ("The legal aid scheme must operate within an overall fixed budget to create a discipline for setting priorities."[8]) This proposal provoked a fierce critical reaction from just about all lawyer and non-lawyer organisations concerned with the provision of legal services, but in July 1996 Lord

[7] *Legal Aid-Targetting Need*, (Cm. 2854, (1995).
[8] *ibid*., Summary, p. viii.

Mackay, in a White Paper,[9] broadly confirmed the plans outlined in the Green Paper.

One of the severest critics of Lord Mackay's proposals at the time was Lord Irvine of Lairg, then Shadow Lord Chancellor. Writing about Lord Mackay's proposals shortly before the 1997 General Election,[10] Lord Irvine quoted extensively from a public lecture I had given in this auditorium at the LSE on today's subject, Access to Justice.[11] He described the lecture as "a devastating attack on the Green Paper"[12] and quoted with approval my conclusion that implementation of the Green Paper "would cause incalculable harm to the legal aid scheme and would seriously diminish access to justice".

However, only a few months after the publication of the essay, Lord Irvine was himself the Lord Chancellor. With little ado[13] he proceeded to implement Lord Mackay's reforms adding for good measure a few further touches of his own, notably the withdrawal of legal aid from personal injury and other damages actions. He announced his plans a mere five months after taking office,[14] and his (one might say ironically entitled), Access to Justice Bill was introduced a year or so later.

Ministers of both this and the previous Government were guilty on too many occasions of making unwarranted and gratuitous criticisms of the legal aid scheme and of legal aid lawyers, probably in the hope of garnering political support for the developing plans to dismantle the scheme. In my judgment,

---

[9] *Striking the Balance*, Cm. 3305 (1996). For reactions to the Green Paper and/or the White Paper see, for instance, *Legal Action*, August, 1996, pp. 1, 8–9; *New Law Journal*, July 5, 1996, p. 977; *Law Society's Gazette*, July 3, 1996, pp. 1, 8; July 10, 1996, pp. 12–13.

[10] Lord Irvine of Lairg, "The Legal System and Law Reform under Labour" in *Law Reform for All*, (D. Bean ed., 1996), pp. 4–29.

[11] Published as "Access to Justice-Towards the 21st Century", in *Law, Society, and Economy* (R. Rawlings, ed., 1997, Clarendon, Oxford), pp. 339–357, see especially pp. 344–348 which were reprinted in *New Law Journal*, July 21, 1995, p. 1098 as "Twelve reasons for rejecting the Legal Aid Green Paper".

[12] *op. cit.*, n. 10 above, at p. 8.

[13] Shortly after taking office in May 1997, Lord Irvine asked a former Treasury mandarin, Sir Peter Middleton, to advise him on legal aid and civil justice reform. Although his report (Sir Peter Middleton, *Review of Civil Justice and Legal Aid*, LCD, September 1997) supported most of Lord Mackay's proposals it suggested that legal aid costs could be brought under control without the need for a cap.

[14] At the Law Society's Annual Conference on October 18, 1997—see *Law Society's Gazette*, October 22, 1997, p. 1 ("Irvine Reforms Slash Legal Aid").

it will soon enough become apparent that the legal aid scheme we had was greatly to be preferred to what will now replace it.

Under the new arrangements legal aid is abolished and the Legal Aid Board which ran the system is replaced by the Legal Services Commission. The Board has deservedly won a fine reputation both for administrative efficiency and for its imaginative approach to the development of publicly funded legal services. My criticisms of the new scheme are in no way directed at the Board which I believe is doing its utmost to make the best of the situation.

The Legal Services Commission, which will take over the Board's existing staff, will operate the system in respect of civil matters through the Community Legal Service (CLS) and in respect of criminal work through the Criminal Defence Service (CDS). The functions of the Commission include assessing local needs for legal services and, having determined priorities in light of directions given by the Lord Chancellor, to match funding to the identified needs. Determining needs in the abstract is obviously a poor alternative to being able to respond to actual needs manifested by real people. There will always be a mismatch between what is planned and what is actually needed.

This would be so even if there were reliable, workable methods of measuring need for legal services. But that is not the situation. Measuring such needs is a fiendishly difficult business and there is no agreed way of proceeding. The Government's recent Consultation Paper on the Community Legal Service, for example, included an appendix purporting to quantify the unmet need for legal services in civil disputes. Having cited various statistics the document concluded, "the figures do not support the proposition that there is a widespread unmet need as a result of inadequate provision"[15]—a verdict that has been greeted by the experts with considerable surprise.[16] On this

---

[15] *The Community Legal Service*, Lord Chancellor's Department, Consultation Paper, May 1999, p. 34.
[16] The National Association of Citizens' Advice Bureaux (NACAB) in its response to the Consultation Paper (July 1999, p. 7) described this conclusion as "premature and probably false". ("It is clear from the volume and nature of enquiries that CABX receive, and the fact that not all enquirers are able to get help quickly enough that there is a substantial amount of unmet need.") The Civil Justice Council in its response (May 1999, p. 6) said it had "great reservation about the analysis". ("All the data used in the analysis is from

topic, a major new study by Professor Hazel Genn (and to which I will return in my lecture next week) is a rather more reliable guide.

But worse, the measuring of need will be done by different agencies using different means and methodologies—by the Legal Services Commission centrally,[17] by each of the Commission's Regional Legal Services Commissions[18] and by the Community Legal Service Partnerships[19] that are being set up all over the country to bring together funders and providers of legal services at the local level. Assessment of unmet need for the Community Legal Service is even to include unscientific surveys in major shops, such as Marks & Spencer, ASDA, Dixons and the like.[20] This does not look like assessment of need in a coherent and consistent way.

The setting of a predetermined annual budget means, by definition, that there must be rationing to ensure that the budget is not overspent. The rationing of legal aid is an attack on access

---

secondary sources, none of which was intended to identify unmet need, nor were they compatible with each other.") See to like effect the response of the Law Society (August 1999, para. 2.19) and of the Legal Action Group (June 1999, pp. 1–5). For the most comprehensive exploration of the problem of unmet need for legal services see now Hazel Genn, *Paths to Justice: What People Do and Think About Going to Law* (Hart Publishing, 1999), especially Chaps 3 and 4.

[17] See in particular Legal Aid Board, Regional Legal Services Committees, *Assessment of Need for Legal Services and Strategies for Contracts to be let in 2000, Overview and Summary of Recommendations*, issued in April 1999. See also the section in the Legal Aid Board's annual report on "Predicting Need for Legal Help" from 1991–1992 onwards.

[18] In its response to the LCD's Consultation Paper on the Community Legal Service, the Law Society said, "the approach to assessing need appears to differ from area to area" (p. vii).

[19] The Consultation Paper on the CLS said that the tasks of the Partnerships (CLSPs) included "Assessing likely levels of need in different parts of the area for information, advice and assistance on different topics" (p. 15). There would be best practice guidance, *inter alia*, on analysing needs and reviewing provision (para. 3.9, p. 13).

[20] In October the Lord Chancellor's Department announced "some of Britain's top high street names are helping to launch the Community Legal Service . . . They have agreed to help find out the sorts of legal problems that people have so that when the Community Legal Service is launched it is focused on the real need of different communities." Staff in the stores would ask shoppers "a small number of simple, carefully designed questions about whether they have faced problems that needed legal solutions and what their experiences were". (LCD, Press Notice, October 8, 1999.)

Justice and Access to Justice

to justice. People who under the old system would have qualified on the means test and the merits test will be denied funding. Even someone who qualifies under the new tests will be denied service if the moneys allocated to that service or that category of work have run out. That is the effect of having a controlled budget.

The real reason for controlling the budget is obviously to placate the Treasury. But the *stated* reasons emphasise rather that it permits the targeting of resources. Thus the Government's White Paper gave as the first objective of the system that it should "direct the available resources to where they are most needed, to reflect defined priorities".[21] It is for this reason that the Lord Chancellor said he had decided to withdraw legal aid from some categories of work, notably personal injury cases.[22] So far the Lord Chancellor has designated two categories of priority.[23] In "top priority" cases the Commission must ensure that all cases are funded. This for the moment consists only of certain proceedings under the Children Act 1989 for which legal aid is available without a means or merits test, and civil proceedings in which the life or liberty of the subject is at stake. Priority is also to be given to housing cases and other "social welfare" cases that enable people to avoid or climb out of social exclusion, domestic violence cases, cases concerning the welfare of children and cases alleging serious wrongdoing, breach of human rights or abuse of position or power by a public body or servant, such as a police officer. This second priority category will be exempt from the new cost-benefit rules for funding which sounds excellent. But it is only an improvement on the previous system if cases in those categories are now to be

---

[21] *Op. cit.*, n. 9 above, at p. 28, para. 3.6.
[22] The excluded categories of work are listed in Schedule 2 to the 1999 Act. They are personal injury negligence cases (other than clinical negligence), conveyancing, boundary disputes, the making of wills, trust law, defamation and malicious falsehood, company or partnership law or other matters arising out of business, and advocacy in proceedings other than those listed in Schedule 2. In exceptional circumstances (which are set out), funding may be given even in the excluded categories—see Legal Aid Board, *A New Approach to Funding Civil Cases*, October 1999, pp. 14–22. As mentioned below (p. 17) the CLS will be able to fund costs of investigation where they are high in order to determine whether funding under a conditional fee agreement (see below) is possible; and also provide partial funding in high cost cases. (*ibid.*, pp. 65–74.)
[23] See the Lord Chancellor's letter in Legal Aid Board, *op. cit.*, n. 22 above, pp. 12–13, and LCD, Press Notice No. 26/00 (February 2, 2000).

funded which previously were not. But where are those cases and by what methods are they going to be found? One method is simply to extend funding to new categories of work previously excluded from legal aid. The Lord Chancellor's very welcome recent decision to extend funding to representation before the immigration appellate authorities is an example. But one imagines there will be few such block extensions.

It has been estimated that the Government's decision to withdraw legal aid from certain categories of work, notably personal injury cases, will save some £35 million.[24] Even in the unlikely event that all that money were allocated to legal services for priority cases, actually getting such cases so that they can be funded is quite a different matter. Moreover, could one rustle up larger numbers of "priority" legal problems without at the same time getting people to come forward in numbers with non-priority legal problems? Quite apart from those practical questions, there is also the question of principle whether taxpayer's money should be used actively to drum up legal work. If that is not the intention I doubt whether the additional moneys notionally allocated to priority cases will in fact be used. A cynic might suggest that that is precisely what the Government hopes will happen.

One major uncertainty amongst many is the extent to which the budget for civil work is at risk of being diminished by the claims of the budget for criminal cases. The Government has taken the point that capping the budget for criminal legal aid would be a breach of the European Convention on Human Rights, Article 6 of which guarantees free representation for those who cannot afford to pay for legal assistance. But there has not as yet been a guarantee of ring-fencing for the civil budget and some of the parliamentary statements on the subject made by ministers during the passage of the Bill were distinctly worrying. During the House of Lords Committee stage, for instance, the Lord Chancellor said, "The only money that is left

---

[24] The savings from announced categories of exclusion from legal aid were calculated as £41 million of which £36 million was due to personal injury cases. £5 million should be deducted from this on account of loss of retained contributions and receipts from the statutory charge. (P. Pleasence *et al.*, *Testing the Code*, The Funding Code-Final Research Report, October 1999, Fig. 53, p. 36.)

for civil legal aid is what is left over out of that budget after the requirements of criminal legal aid have been met."[25]

Hitherto, *all* solicitors' firms have been able to undertake legal aid work. In future only those that have contracts from the Legal Services Commission will be permitted to do so.[26] The effect of this will be to drastically reduce the number of outlets providing the service from around 11,000 to some 5,000 to 6,000. One can expect clients to travel a certain distance to get advice and help with legal problems, but to more than halve the number of firms able to do publicly funded work is bound to have a harmful effect on the accessibility of legal services for many clients, and not only in rural areas.

In future there may not be more than a single contracted firm in a locality available to do particular categories of work. The Legal Aid Board said in April 1998 that in regard to Family Law, for instance, most centres of population of any significance should have "at least one contracted firm with a second contracted firm within reasonable proximity".[27] So smaller centres of population might not have more than one contracted practitioner to do Family Law work which is mainstream work for most solicitors' firms. Presumably in less mainstream areas of work there might only be a single contracted firm even in centres of significant population. Quite apart from the serious effect of the reduction in points of access for potential clients, the power of patronage wielded by the Legal Services Commission in deciding who does and who does not get a contract is frightening. The idea that bureaucracy will determine who can provide legal services and where is not a happy one.

The allocation of contracts through block grants will be subject to competitive tendering. The December 1998 White Paper stated that contracting would "promote better value for

---

[25] *Hansard*, H.L. Vol. 596, col. 918, January 26, 1999. The Solicitor General said in the Commons Committee stage, "The hon. member for Beaconsfield raised Art. 6 [of the European Convention], which might become a pressure in the context of the Criminal Defence Service budget. However, it is necessary to set budgets." (House of Commons, Standing Committee "E", April 29, 1999, col. 83.)

[26] As from January 1, 2000, advice and assistance under the Green Form scheme—to be known in future as "Legal Help"—can only be provided by contracted providers. A rolling programme will bring all other publicly funded legal services into the contracted system by 2003.

[27] Response to Lord Chancellor's Consultation Paper on Exclusive Contracting, April 1998, p. 26, para. 3.27.

money by providing the basis for competition and by fixing prices in a way that encourages greater efficiency".[28] The obvious risk is that standards of service will decline since, whatever protestations are made about insistence on quality of work, the natural tendency will be to accept the lowest bids. Lord Irvine made the point when he was Shadow Lord Chancellor. Labour, he said, was against competitive tendering "because of the inevitable tendency to favour low-price against higher-quality bidders".[29] The Legal Aid Board Research Unit has warned that American experience showed that competitive bidding created an incentive to weigh cost over quality. Contrary to the rhetoric, cost tended to go up whilst quality went down. Fixed price contracts resulted in case overload, less than adequate representation for clients, and instability as contractors were replaced from year to year. It also involved heavy administrative costs to process bids and negotiate contracts.[30]

The decision whether a particular client gets state funding for a civil case will be based first, as previously, on a means test, but the traditional merits test will be replaced by the new Funding Code. The old test was simple and was the same for all cases. (In essence, were there reasonable prospects of success and was it reasonable in all the circumstances that public money be used for the case?) Under the new Funding Code there will be a different test for different types of case. The draft Code said:

> "Rather than attempting to apply one universal test to a huge variety of civil cases, the new Funding Code has the flexibility to apply different criteria to different types of case."[31]

It described the old test as "vague and subjective". Instead the new test would be "clear and objective" with "specific criteria in terms of prospects of success, costs and damages".[32]

---

[28] *op. cit.*, n. 9 above, at para. 3.18.
[29] *op.cit.*, n. 10 above, at p. 10.
[30] P. Pleasence *et al.*, "Profiling Civil Litigation: The case for research", Legal Aid Board Research Unit (1996), pp. 93–94. In 1998–1999 the Board spent £3.7 million in managing 2,725 suppliers or £1,385 per supplier. (Legal Aid Board's Response to the LCD's Consultation Paper on the Community Legal Service, September 1999, p. 24, para. 3.10.) Obviously, negotiating contracts and managing and auditing providers under the new system will involve considerably more work.
[31] Legal Aid Board, *The Funding Code*, (January 1999), p. 2.
[32] *ibid.*, p. 5.

Justice and Access to Justice

Where the claim is for quantifiable damages, the Code will specify percentage bands of success and minimum cost/benefit ratios. So where prospects of success are Very Good (80 per cent or better), likely damages must exceed likely costs. Where prospects are Good (60–80 per cent), likely damages will have to exceed costs by at least 2:1. Where prospects are only Fair (50–60 per cent), damages will have to exceed costs by at least 4:1.

The Legal Aid Board's own recently published research shows that these cost/benefit requirements will mean that a very significant proportion of cases now funded by legal aid will no longer get funding. They estimate that about a fifth of legally aided cases with very good prospects of success (80 per cent plus), and over half the non-housing cases in the good prospects of success (60–80 per cent) category and in the moderate (50–60 per cent) bracket would not qualify.[33] Those figures are very alarming. Moreover, the weight to be given to the new cost/benefit assessment seems wholly disproportionate given that there cannot be any exactitude about percentage estimates of success, nor of likely costs,[34] nor of likely damages. The suggestion that the new criteria are "clear and objective" where the old test was "vague and subjective" is therefore unconvincing. In fact the new criteria are considerably more open to different interpretations than the simple old test, if only because of their immense complexity and of the number of factors that will have to be taken into account. The draft Funding Code said that the new structured approach using minimum cost or damage threshholds and ratios "should encourage more consistency in decision taking". I would say the exact opposite is the case.

Also under the new system solicitors will have to take into consideration whether they can afford to take the case having regard to its likely cost in the light of the firm's block grant. Firms will be tempted to favour cases that maximise their profit margin—thus creating a new conflict of interest problem between the client and the lawyer.

---

[33] Legal Aid Board, *A New Approach to Funding Civil Cases*, (October 1999), pp. 51–52.

[34] Research published by the Legal Aid Board in October 1999 showed that solicitor cost predictions were inaccurate in 60 per cent of cases. See P. Pleasence *et al.*, *Testing the Code*, Legal Aid Board Research Report (October 1999), p. 30.

A person unable to get state funded legal services, and not rich enough to afford to fund the case himself, may now look to finance his case by way of a conditional fee or "no win—no fee" agreement, under which the solicitor agrees that if the case is lost he will not charge the client, whereas if it is won he will charge a success fee calculated as a percentage of his costs. Under a conditional fee agreement (CFA), if the client wins the case, his solicitor gets his normal fees paid by the loser. On top of that he can charge his own client the agreed success fee which can be anything up to 100 per cent of his costs—subject to the proviso that the Law Society recommends that the lawyer should not take more than 25 per cent of the client's damages. (It is not clear whether this 25 per cent cap will survive.)

CFAs, which have been allowed only since 1995, have been used mainly for personal injury cases. Solicitor members of the Law Society's Personal Injury Panel, for what at least started as a modest premium, could additionally offer their clients insurance cover against the risk of losing and therefore having to pay the other side's costs.[35] Recently the premiums have gone up sharply and are no longer quite so attractive.[36]

When Lord Irvine announced in 1997 that legal aid was to be withdrawn from personal injury cases and that claimants would instead have to look for funding to conditional fee agreements, the critics pointed to the danger that some claimants would not be able to find a solicitor willing to take their case on a conditional fee basis or, alternatively, that the insurance premium to cover the risk of losing might be prohibitively high. The Lord Chancellor contended that viable cases would find a willing solicitor and that the insurance industry would market after-the-event insurance policies at sensible premiums to cater for most viable cases. The critics accused him of being naively over-optimistic. However, Lord Irvine then came forward with an unexpected response to the problem. The Access to Justice Act 1999 provides that both the success fee and the insurance premium paid to cover the risk of losing are recoverable by the

---

[35] In 1995, the premium was £85 for all claims. Subsequently the cost rose slightly for road traffic cases and rather more for other claims.
[36] The rise was from £92 to £148 for road traffic cases and from £155 to £315 for other claims. See *Law Society's Gazette*, October 13, 1999, p. 1.

winner from the loser.[37] When this is brought into effect next April it will resolve some of the concerns over CFAs.

However, there will still be a variety of situations where great problems will remain. One is when the client cannot find lawyers willing to act on a CFA even though it is a winnable case. Solicitors may, for instance, demand an unreasonably high chance of success before being willing to take on the case. Another is where there is no funding to pay the insurance premium. Many solicitors' firms, and especially smaller firms, may find it impossible to advance substantial insurance premiums, or for that matter even fairly modest premiums, for large numbers of clients.[38] Another is when no insurance cover can be arranged, for instance because insurers have stopped covering that firm because its average success rate has slipped below some required percentage imposed by the insurance company. (Control over litigation exercised by insurance companies will increase enormously as a result of the growth of CFAs.) Another is where the client is being asked to pay disbursements that he cannot afford. Paying your own disbursements is the norm under CFAs.[39] (It has recently been announced that in heavy personal injury cases or when a great deal of investigation is needed the Legal Services Commission will be able to pay part of the costs including the insurance premium and disbursements. This is very welcome news but it will apply only to a small minority of cases.[40])

---

[37] ss. 27(6) and 29. The resulting issues are canvassed in *Conditional Fees: Sharing the Risks of Litigation*, LCD Consultation Paper, (September 1999). The Paper suggested that the other party should have early notification of the existence of a CFA and of an insurance policy covering the CFA but not of the level of the success fee or of the insurance premium. See now LCD, Press Notice No. 24/00 (February 1, 2000).

[38] For an assessment of the financial implications for firms of CFAs see J. Shapland *et al.*, *Affording Civil Justice*, Law Society Research Study No. 29 (1998).

[39] Research on CFAs has shown that in over three-quarters of cases clients were funding their own disbursements. See S. Yarrow, *The Price of Success: lawyers, clients and conditional fees*, Policy Studies Institute (1997), p. 59.

[40] Where the disbursements are likely to be over £5,000 or the costs over £15,000 the case will be eligible for "litigation support" under which the Commission will cover costs above those threshhold figures in return for a proportionate share of the success fee. Where the disbursements are likely to be over £1,000 or costs over £3,000 at the initial stages, the case will be eligible for "investigation support". See Legal Aid Board, *A New Approach to Funding Civil Cases*, (October 1999), pp. 67–69 as amended, see LCD, Press Notice No. 26/00 (February 2, 2000).

Justice and Access to Justice

The Civil Justice Council giving its verdict on the Government's proposals said, "We are concerned that funding plans appear to rely heavily on CFAs and insurance to fill significant gaps in provision. Such assumptions are premature."[41]

Certainly, the overall effect of making success fees and insurance premiums recoverable will obviously be to increase the cost of litigation for losing defendants—which, no doubt, will be reflected soon enough in higher insurance premiums for us all. It is equally predictable that the level of both success fees and premiums for insurance policies to cover CFAs will rise, which would have a further inflationary effect on the costs of litigation and would, incidentally, bring solicitors undeserved windfall profits from CFAs.[42] The loser will have the right to ask for a review of the level of both the success fee and of the premium, but it may not be easy to establish that the lawyer's early estimate of risk was too high. Also, challenge of the level of the success fee and of the insurance premium will in practice generally not occur in cases that settle (as, of course, most do).

The overall impact of CFAs on the economics of litigation will therefore be very great. Among the many wholly unpredictable issues is to what extent changes in the pattern of funding through the withdrawal of legal aid and the development of CFAs will bring in new clients.[43]

Another unpredictable feature of the new funding arrangements under the Access to Justice Act is what impact will be made by the new initiatives to be taken by the Community Legal Service (CLS).[44] To judge from the emphasis it has given them, the Government apparently regards these as very important. The overwhelming bulk of CLS expenditure (of the order of some £800 million) will obviously go, as before, in providing the services of solicitors and barristers in private practice, above all in family law matters—though now it will be under the new contractual arrangements. Expenditure on the new initiatives

---

[41] "The Community Legal Service: A Consultation Paper", LCD (May 1999), p. 8.
[42] Research showed an average success fee in personal injury cases of 43 per cent (*op. cit.*, n. 39 above, at p. 57). Considering the risk of losing in personal injury cases, this seems high. See further M.C. Hemsworth, "Conditional fee agreements and litigation funding", *New Law Journal*, November 5, 1999, p. 1660.
[43] The first published research on CFAs said, "The results of this survey do not give a firm answer to this question." (Yarrow, *op. cit.*, n. 39 above, at p. 91.)
[44] The LCD's Consultation Paper on the CLS of May 1999 must be read together with the Legal Aid Board's Response of September 1999. Information on developments can also be found on the Community Legal Service website.

Justice and Access to Justice

will by comparison be minuscule. It was announced recently with fanfares that of the annual £200 million plus expenditure on Green Form advice and assistance (in future to be known as "Legal Help"), £20 million will be reserved for contracting by the CLS with the not-for-profit sector—a relatively modest sum hardly any of which in fact is new money.[45]

Given the balance of funding between the private and the not-for-profit sector, it is strange verging on bizarre that in the Consultation Paper on the Community Legal Service and in the innumerable statements about the CLS made by Government ministers there has hardly been a mention of the basic mainstream function of funding work done by private practitioners.[46] All the emphasis has been on the fancy new aspects of the service with the not-for-profit sector.

A recent speech by the Lord Chancellor summarised the main themes: "The Community Legal Service", he said, "is the first attempt ever by any government to deliver legal services in a joined up way. It will provide a framework for comprehensive local networks of good quality legal and advice services supported by coordinated funding, and based on the needs of local people."[47]

A variety of initiatives are being taken to promote the concept of what are grandly being called "joined up" legal services. One is the establishment of a CLS website with the aim of assisting both providers of advice and those of their clients who have access to the Internet. It will be particularly valuable to people who because of disability or distance cannot easily reach an advice centre. The Internet can be used to disseminate information about available facilities, about legal problems and about

---

[45] Some £12 million is currently being paid to 170 or so advice agencies; about £3 million is paid by way of Green Form legal advice and assistance to law centres and a few advice agencies; and some £2 million has been allocated to the new Methods of Delivery pilot study—see n. 51 below.

[46] The Legal Action Group's Response to the Consultation Paper on the Community Legal Service (p. 1, para. 1.4) described it as "insubstantial and inadequate",

("There are no detailed proposals in the paper, which ignores the role of solicitors in private practice, and has virtually no reference to representation or to litigation. None of the 47 organisations visited by the LCD was a firm of solicitors in private practice, and of the 75 organisations the LCD had meetings with, only one was. There is no reference to the role of the legal aid funded provision within the CLS or to the consequences of moving to exclusive contracting for legal aid.")

[47] Speech at County Hall, Truro, October 15, 1999.

how to handle them.[48] In the short term the website will be stronger in providing information than in giving advice. In the longer run it may develop expert systems or intelligent checklists enabling at least the more skilled and the more intelligent to obtain "do-it-yourself" advice.

With Internet access spreading rapidly, these developments are to be welcomed. However, for some time to come it will probably remain the case that Internet access will be heavily affected by class differences. (A recent survey showed that whereas a third of people in classes A and B had access to the Internet at home, the proportion for classes D and E was only 2 per cent.[49]) Also, the fact that one has access to the web at home does not mean that one either feels able or is competent to use it even just for the purpose of seeking information about legal problems (as opposed to booking a holiday), let alone for the much more demanding task of trying to get advice or assistance. (I speak with feeling as someone who still has not fully mastered the art of programming a video recorder.)

The Internet is not the only way of deploying information technology in this field. Public access terminals using interactive video technology in court foyers or libraries seem to be a useful and cost-effective way of providing information and guidance. One advantage is that such information can be provided in different languages. But again many of the most vulnerable have poor literacy skills and will not be well placed to take advantage of such aids.

Apart from the use of information technology, the CLS is planning to develop a variety of alternative approaches to promoting access to help with legal problems, for instance, through telephone, mobile and other services, including specialist second-tier advice services provided to advisers.[50] So, for instance, a pilot scheme starting in 2000 will make free specialist help available over the telephone to solicitors and advice agencies in the fields of social welfare law, immigration and

---

[48] See especially R. Susskind, *The Future of Law Facing the Challenges of Information Technology*, (Clarendon, Oxford, 1996). Professor Susskind is the LCD's adviser on IT.

[49] A Guardian/ICM poll in January 1999 cited in *The Community Legal Service, A Consultation Paper*, LCD (May 1999), p. 22, para. 5.6.

[50] For a report on research commissioned by the Legal Aid Board see J. Steele and J. Seargeant, *Access to legal services: The contribution of alternative approaches* (Policy Studies Institute, 1999).

human rights.[51] The Legal Aid Board has for some years been exploring ways of bringing the not-for-profit advice sector into the scheme for providing help with legal problems. This is an important aspect of the plans for the Community Legal Service.

The task of co-ordination of the different systems for helping citizens with their legal problems will fall to the new CLS Partnerships. These partnerships will be between the CLS, local government and other funders of advisory services together with representatives of the providers of services. As has already been noted, the partnerships are supposed to identify the level of unmet need for legal services and they are supposed then to map existing provision of services and to devise improved networks to plug gaps in local provision and better referral systems to ensure that the person with the problem reaches the appropriate adviser. Six pioneer areas are testing out the Partnership concept and 40 other local authorities are involved as Associate Pioneers.[52] Local initiative is to be encouraged but best practice guidance will be circulated in the hope of promoting it on a nationwide basis.

These plans sound promising, but they raise many questions. Since there is no compulsion on local authorities to participate effectively or at all, how can reluctant authorities be made to play their part?[53] Equally, how can local authorities that are currently funding legal services be prevented from withdrawing or reducing such funding when they see that central government moneys are now to be available?[54] The best way might be to put local authorities under a statutory obligation to fund advice provision similar to the duty under the Housing Act 1996

---

[51] In addition to telephone advice, complex cases could be referred. The experts providing the service include Shelter, Liberty and the Joint Council for the Welfare of Immigrants. The outreach service will allow advice to be given at venues such as doctors surgeries, libraries and other advice agencies. The pilot will run for 12–15 months. See Legal Aid Board, *Focus*, No. 27, (September 1999), p. 10.

[52] For details of the areas see the LCD's Consultation Paper, *The Community Legal Service* (May 1999), p. 13. For further information see the CLS's website.

[53] The Legal Aid Board's response to the Consultation Paper on the CLS said, "there remains the possibility that individual local authorities will decide not to enter into partnership arrangements with the [Legal Services] Commission" (September 1999), p. ii, para. 8.)

[54] Local authorities are a major funder of legal services through grants to advice agencies and law centres. The level of funding is unclear. The Consultation Paper on the Community Legal Service suggested a figure of over £150 million a year (p. 33, para. B4).

Justice and Access to Justice

to provide advice and information about homelessness free of charge.[55]

Again, how likely is that different funders will be able to agree on who is to provide and to pay for particular services? The Legal Aid Board says that each local partnership "will form a funding group which will make the final recommendations on funding within each partnership arrangement for final approval by the relevant individual funding bodies".[56] But since each funding body will be able to take its own decisions, will the talk of co-ordinated funding amount to much? It is difficult to imagine different providers working for different agencies agreeing on rationalisation of the services where that means elimination or downgrading of their own activities.

What, for that matter, does rationalisation actually mean? To take an example, how does the plan for a CLS website providing information fit with the new Citizens' Advice Bureaux Adviceguide website?[57] The number of users of this new CAB service reached 2,000 a week shortly after its launch and is expected to grow rapidly. The National Association of Citizens' Advice Bureaux is currently exploring with other organisations of the Advice Services Alliance, the possibility of a joint initiative to ensure that there is a single point of access to reliable, up-to-date and accurate information which avoids duplication and makes effective use of resources. It would be extremely unfortunate if the plans for these two national systems were not synchronised but it is easier to speak of co-ordination than to achieve it.[58]

Another large question is how gaps in service provision can be filled if there is no new money. There are, for instance, some 50 law centres. Supposing assessment of need suggested that another 50 were required, is it conceivable that the money would be forthcoming to set them up? Obviously not. Then

---

[55] s. 179(1).
[56] Legal Aid Board's Response to the LCD's Consultation Paper on the Community Legal Service (September 1999), para. 2.81.
[57] This will offer information both on terminals in CAB waiting rooms, libraries and similar facilities and 24-hour access from personal computers at home. (www.adviceguide.org.uk).
[58] The Legal Aid Board's response to the LCD's Consultation Paper on the Community Legal Service, referring to the NACAB's website and other website developments, said, "Pooling expertise and learning from others' experience (including from elsewhere in the world) will be important to realising longer term objectives". (September 1999, p. vi, para. 24.)

again, how will the Community Legal Service be able to avoid unacceptable differences in levels of service at the local level.[59] On the other hand, trying to even out provision by the transfer of moneys from one area to another, or from one service to another means, by definition, that need that is currently being met would no longer be met. There is no way of squaring this circle.

The Consultation Paper says that in order to achieve proper referral between advisers and the most effective deployment of resources in a particular area, "it will be very important for formal working agreements or concordats to be drawn up among all the various bodies involved in each area. These will set out standing arrangements for their mutual co-operation in the advice they give and the services they provide".[60] My concern is that these "formal working agreements or concordats" for referral may become rigid new demarcation lines that work to the client's disadvantage. Having elaborate arrangements designed to direct clients with legal problems to the "right" adviser may actually be counter-productive.

At present there is a wide range of choice. Lawyers in private practice and in law centres, CABs, consumer advice centres, housing aid centres, neighbourhood centres, can all make a contribution to sorting out people's legal problems.[61] The College of Law has just announced that it plans to establish a nationwide network of free legal advice clinics staffed by students under the supervision of practitioners and teachers.[62] I

---

[59] In its response to the Consultation Paper on the CLS the Legal Aid Board has said, "It is entirely appropriate that the services available through the CLS should vary between regions according to local needs, in fact it is difficult to see how the services could be responsive to local needs and priorities if they did not". But it followed this by saying that the CLS' services would be provided "on a consistent basis reflecting local needs and priorities". (September 1999, p. 9, paras 2.26–2.27.)

[60] *op. cit.*, n. 52 above, at p. 15.

[61] The Consultation Paper on the CLS stated,

> "A significant number of lawyers and others working in independent advice centres, Citizens' Advice Bureaux (CABx) and Law Centres, provide this vital initial advice. This effort is on a scale without rival anywhere in the world . . . It involves nearly 6,000 professional staff and some 30,000 unpaid volunteers working in over 3,000 centres dealing with over 10 million enquiries each year. Total public funding . . . is probably about £250 million a year." (May 1999, pp. 1–2).

[62] See *Law Society's Gazette*, October 27, 1999, p. 3.

see no reason why that should not also play a part. The great variety of overlapping potential sources of information, advice and assistance is an enormous benefit to the citizen with the problem. It would be churlish to be against mutual co-operation and better communication between agencies or even greater efficiency in referral systems. If that achieves a better balance between generalist and specialist agencies in a locality and the filling of gaps in the provision of services, so much the better. But formal working agreements or concordats between agencies could stifle rather than facilitate.

The crucial factor in all of this is that there will be no additional money for legal services. Without new resources it will be difficult to achieve anything of great consequence beyond re-arranging the deckchairs. Will worthwhile amounts of money actually become available for re-allocation to new legal services uses and, if so, will those new uses turn out to be a better application of public money? The fact that the project is being written up by politicians in glowing terms, that there are attractive champions to blow the trumpet,[63] that some enthusiasm is being generated and that valiant preparatory work is being done does not establish that it will. Certainly there are some interesting developments that could bear worthwhile fruit, but the plans for the Community Legal Service are still vague and incoherent.[64] For the moment I prefer to reserve judgment as to whether the potential gains from the new arrangements will compensate in any way for the certain losses. I fear they will not.

The truth is that the Government's reforms spring not from a desire to improve access to justice but from the Treasury's need to control the budget. The entire new system flows from the decision to cap the budget. This will infect the whole enterprise. The point was seen by Lord Irvine himself, writing when he was still in Opposition:

[63] A number of public figures, including media personalities such as Esther Rantzen and Jenni Murray, have been named by the Lord Chancellor as CLS "champions". See *Law Society's Gazette*, October 6, 1999, p. 4.
[64] The Civil Justice Council said of the May 1999 Consultation Paper on the CLS that it was "too short on detail and too silent in major areas of the CLS's work to be adequate". Among the vital questions that were not addressed were "who will have access to the community legal services, what levels of need must be met, how much will central government contribute, what is the minimum level of service provision required in any area" (p. 8). The Consultation Paper, it said, lacked a strategic plan for the whole of the CLS.

> "Capping signifies an abandonment of an entitlement basis for the grant of legal aid, based on merits . . . Legal aid will cease to be a benefit to which the individual who qualifies is entitled. It will in practice become a discretionary benefit, available at bureaucratic disposal—a benefit which will have to be disallowed when the money runs out, or when another category of cases has been given funding preference."

Lord Irvine alluded to the arguments put forward by the Conservative Government and the Legal Aid Board to allay fears as to how the new system would work:

> "There is much sophistry about the contracts with the suppliers being for different periods, and long periods, so that no one in practice need be excluded."

That, he said, was not persuasive.

> "Capping is crude. Legal aid will cease to be a service available on an equal basis nationally. Cases will go forward in one region where identical cases in others, of equal merit, will not because of capping. In practice capping will lead at worst to substantial exclusion from justice and at best to long waiting lists. Typically legal aid is sought at times of crisis for the individual. Its availability should not depend on the accident of where the individual lives or when application is made."

My sentiments precisely.

2. Civil Justice

Civil justice concerns the handling of disputes between citizens arising out of civil, as opposed to criminal, law. The phrase is normally used to signify all stages of civil disputes by *courts*, including the issue of proceedings, settlement, trial and post-trial appeals. In recent years what is defined as civil justice has been broadened to include also a variety of other systems for resolving disputes lumped together as Alternative Dispute Resolution or ADR.

The subject has attracted much attention of late around the world. In this jurisdiction we have had Lord Woolf's famous reports on *Access to Justice*[1] implemented as a wide-ranging package of reforms as from last April. But the Woolf report was only the latest in a long line of such reports. There have been over 60 official reports on the subject of civil process in the past 100 years, and no fewer than five since the Second World War—the Evershed Report in 1953,[2] the Report of the Winn Committee in 1968,[3] the Cantley Working Party in 1979,[4] the Civil Justice Review in the late 1980s[5] and then Woolf. The focus of such reports is always the same—how to reduce the complexity, delay and cost of civil litigation. It seems that this is a subject that refuses to go away. It is safe to predict that the Woolf report will not be the last on the subject.

---

[1] *Interim Report*, 1995; *Final Report*, 1996.
[2] *Final Report of the Committee on Supreme Court Practice and Procedure*, Cmd. 8878 (1953).
[3] *Committee on Personal Injury Litigation*, Cmnd. 369 (1968).
[4] *Report of the Personal Injuries Litigation Procedure Working Party*, Cmnd. 7476 (1979).
[5] In 1985–1986 the Review produced five Consultation Papers on Personal Injuries, Small Claims, Commercial Court, Enforcement of Debt and Housing Cases. In 1987, it produced its *General Issues Paper* and in 1988, its final report, *Report of the Review Body on Civil Justice*, Cm. 394 (1988).

Given the amount of official concern about the problem of civil justice it is striking that there is so much about the subject that we do not know. Whether one looks at scholarly writing, empirical research or official statistics, criminal justice is much better served than civil justice. Most university law faculties have several courses on aspects of criminal justice. There are hardly any courses anywhere on civil justice. The subject has been curiously neglected.[6]

One thing we do know is that the disputes that reach a court for decision are a tiny fraction of the total number of civil disputes and that most civil disputes do not even reach the level of being formal claims. To take one illustration, in 1984 the Oxford Socio-Legal Centre published a study of over 1,700 accidents where in every case the victim had suffered physical impairment lasting for two or more weeks. Only one in seven (14 per cent) made a claim, one in eight (12 per cent) obtained damages; there were a mere five cases out of 1,711 that were decided in a contested hearing by a court.[7]

A pictorial representation of civil disputes is like a pyramid with the base representing the mass of disputes and the apex representing the tiny proportion that reach a court, with the body of the pyramid representing the infinite variety of ways in which such problems are dealt with by citizens with or without advice from others and whether or not involving legal proceedings. The civil justice system is brought into play in only a small proportion of all these disputes. So the great and continuing preoccupation with reforming the system is energy applied to a very small portion of the total mass of civil justice problems in the community.

Before a situation becomes a formal claim based on law the victim has to appreciate that the law provides a possible remedy for what happened which he then decides to pursue.[8] If the person with the potential remedy is unaware of that fact, he obviously will do nothing about it. But even if the victim of the

---

[6] See Hazel Genn, "Understanding Civil Justice" *Current Legal Problems* (1994), pp. 155–188. For an exploration of many of the problems of the subject see Sir Jack Jacob, *The Fabric of English Civil Justice*, (Hamlyn Lecture of 1986).

[7] D. Harris *et al*, *Compensation and Support for Illness and Injury* (Clarendon, Oxford, 1984), pp. 51, 112.

[8] See W. Felstiner *et al.*, "The Emergence and Transformation of Disputes: Naming, Blaming and Claiming" in *Law and Society Review* (1981, Vol. 15), p. 631.

occurrence realises that there is something that might be done, it by no means follows that he will do anything about it. There are a great many factors that can lead to a decision not to take action, including pessimism about getting the evidence to prove the case; fear of the cost; fear of the ordeal of giving evidence in court combined with ignorance that few cases reach the court; ignorance of the law—for instance that one's own negligence does not necessarily preclude an action; unwillingness to take action that might disrupt a continuing relationship, for instance, between landlord and tenant, employer and employee or in a business relationship[9]; concern over the delay involved; a sense of hopelessness; or a feeling that the cause is not sufficiently serious to justify the effort, the worry and the bother.

By a happy coincidence, the most sophisticated study of these issues to date has just been published by Professor Hazel Genn of University College, London.[10] The 260-page study, funded by the Nuffield Foundation, was based on screening interviews in their homes with a random national sample of over 4,000 individuals aged 18 or over, followed by face-to-face interviews with over 1,100 of the sample who had been identified as having experienced a non-trivial justiciable problem in the previous five years. The social class profile of the main sample was close to that of the general population.[11]

Having indicated that they had experienced one or more of various types of legal problems the respondents were asked a series of questions about what, if anything, they had done about the matter. Only five per cent[12] said they did nothing at all. Those who took no action were most likely to have experienced problems relating to money, accidental injury or work-related ill-health, employment, clinical negligence or unfair action by the police. These are hardly minor matters. Unsurprisingly, they were disproportionately likely to have low incomes and to have no or poor educational qualifications. They were also significantly less likely to have sought advice for previous problems.[13]

---

[9] For an illuminating discussion of this phenomenon see, for instance, Hugh Collins, *Regulating Contracts*, (OUP, 1999), Chap. 14.

[10] I was grateful to Professor Genn for making a copy of the report available to me in advance of publication. H. Genn, *Paths to Justice, What People Do and Think about Going to Law* (Hart Publishing, 1999).

[11] For details of the statistical representativeness of the sample see Tables 2.7, 2.8, at pp. 57–58.

[12] In all statistics drawn from the study by Professor Genn, n = the 1,134 persons in the "main sample".

[13] *ibid.*, pp. 69, 72.

However, 95 per cent did make some attempt to deal with the problem. Mostly this consisted of trying to take it up with the person directly responsible such as the landlord, the employer or the retailer. Sometimes this produced a result, sometimes it did not. The success rate varied from one problem area to another.[14]

Overall, just over one third (34 per cent) of all the respondents resolved the problem by agreement.[15] (A little under half of them had had some form of advice.[16])

In 14 per cent of cases the matter was resolved by adjudication of some kind whether by a court, a tribunal or an ombudsman. Whilst there were far more people in the sample who initiated the case than had a case brought against them, amongst those who had some form of adjudication it was the other way round.[17]

So, in just over half the cases no result was achieved. Apart from the few who, as has been seen, did nothing, some abandoned the matter without taking advice, some abandoned it after taking advice and a few abandoned it after taking legal proceedings.[18] In about half those cases the matter seemed to have reached some form of closure, at least in the sense that it was no longer current. In the rest it was still current but usually the respondent said he did not intend to pursue it further, typically because there seemed nothing else to do, or it would cost too much or the respondent was fed up with the problem or had had enough of trying to sort it out.[19]

---

[14] ibid., Fig. 6.7, p. 197.

[15] ibid., Fig. 5.1, p. 147.

[16] ibid., Fig. 5.1, pp. 147, 148. (14 per cent resolved the matter by agreement without advice; 17 per cent resolved it by agreement after advice but without legal proceedings; and 3 per cent resolved it by agreement after having advice and starting legal proceedings but there was no hearing.)

[17] There were 962 in the sample who had taken the initiative as compared with 160 who had action taken against them (ibid., Fig. 5.4, p. 153). Among respondents who said they had action taken against them, 69 per cent were involved in legal proceedings; among those who were initiating the matter, only 13 per cent were involved in legal proceedings. There was an actual hearing in 56 per cent of the former category and 9 per cent of the latter category (ibid., p. 151).

[18] ibid., p. 148. 5 per cent did nothing; 16 per cent abandoned the matter without having had advice; 30 per cent abandoned it after having had advice and without starting legal proceedings; and 3 per cent abandoned it after starting legal proceedings. For discussion of the reasons for not taking advice about pursuing the matter, see pp. 75–76.

[19] ibid., pp. 148–49.

In trying to understand what the figures mean in terms of unmet need, the proportion seeking and obtaining advice is obviously significant. Just over half the sample (51 per cent) took advice of some sort.[20] But it would be wrong to jump to the conclusion that the other half did not know how to go about seeking advice. As many as four-fifths of all the respondents were aware of the existence of Citizens' Advice Bureaux[21] and more than nine out of ten (91 per cent) people interviewed had received advice from some adviser in the past to help resolve other matters. As many as 68 per cent of the whole sample had previously taken legal advice.[22] Of those in the sample who took no advice on this occasion, four out of five (81 per cent) had previously taken advice.[23]

The fact that most people seem to know about the existence of Citizens' Advice Bureaux is especially important as they provide a great nationwide, free information and advice service and plans for the Government's Community Legal Service rightly give them a central role. (In 1997–98 the Bureaux dealt with over 6.2 million problems.) It is also very significant that the survey shows that Bureaux are used extensively by all income groups, other than those with incomes of £41,000 or more.[24]

When those who had considered seeking advice from solicitors or a Citizens' Advice Bureau or other adviser had not done so, typically it was because they thought that nothing could be done about the problem or that it would involve too much trouble or would be too expensive. In some cases it was because the problem was resolved before contact was made. I suspect that probably not a great deal can be done to reduce those reasons for not taking advice.[25] Some of those who had not taken advice reported practical problems, such as the limited opening hours of Citizens' Advice Bureaux, the waiting time to

---

[20] Fig. 5.1, p. 147. (In 17 per cent the matter was successfully resolved by agreement following advice; in 3 per cent the matter was successfully resolved by agreement after legal proceedings were started; in 12 per cent the matter was concluded by adjudication after advice; and in 19 per cent there was advice but no resolution of the matter.)
[21] ibid., p. 76.
[22] ibid., p. 68.
[23] ibid., p. 72. Among those who did nothing, 56 per cent had previously taken advice; among those who did something but who took no advice, 50 per cent said they had sought advice from a CAB on previous occasions. (ibid., p. 76.)
[24] ibid., pp. 86–87.
[25] ibid., p. 75.

get an appointment, difficulty in making telephone contact to arrange an appointment, congestion and therefore queues in the office and such like.[26] Such problems could be addressed if sufficient funds were there to expand the service, but whether that will prove possible must be doubtful.

For anyone who thinks that in a well-ordered system a good proportion of people with legal problems ought to be using legal proceedings, Professor Genn's study will be discouraging. In about eight out of ten problems in the sample no legal proceedings were begun, no ombudsman was contacted and no Alternative Dispute Resolution method was used.

In summary therefore, what emerges is that, first, most people with legal problems do *something* to resolve them, if only to complain; secondly, very few of them use the official civil justice system despite the fact that they know about taking advice from Citizens' Advice Bureaux and solicitors and, thirdly, that most give up without getting any form of resolution of the matter.

Is this a good thing or a bad thing? That is a crucial question but it is not one to which there is an easy answer. Professor Genn did not attempt to make a judgment as to whether respondents were sensible in their decision to pursue or not to pursue the matter. (She did discover, however, that over two-thirds of all the respondents said they did not regret anything about their handling of the problem.[27])

Whether one thinks that a person *should* involve him or herself in legal proceedings can only be answered sensibly in the context of a particular situation with knowledge of the full facts. How important is the matter to the individual? What would be involved in terms of time, cost and stress in trying to get it resolved? If a widow with small children says that she did not claim in respect of the death of her husband killed in the course of his employment because "she couldn't be bothered" or she was worried about having to go to court or she didn't know how to proceed, everyone would agree that the failure to

---

[26] *ibid.*, pp. 76–77.

[27] The problems with the highest proportion of regrets were divorce and separation problems, problems with landlords and employment disputes. Those with the fewest regrets were neighbour problems and money problems. This is despite the fact that divorce and separation had a high resolution rate, whilst neighbour problems had a low resolution rate (*ibid.*, p. 204). There was no breakdown showing regrets by whether, and if so, how, the matter was resolved.

act was, to say the least, problematic. Given the gravity of the situation and the value of the potential claim, the reason given would be an insufficient justification for inaction. She ought to have done something to pursue the matter. Something or someone must be at fault for her failure to do so. To take an opposite extreme case, if a businessman who has spent good money on having lawyers draw up a contract, decides to sort out a problem arising out of the contract over a drink rather than bringing in his legal advisers, one takes an entirely different view. He can be expected to know where his best interests lie and if he chooses not to utilise the legal system, why would one object? Or, to take examples that could affect any of us, if, "couldn't be bothered" or "it isn't worthwhile" applies to the common irritations of ordinary life—the defective moderately costly consumer item, the collision that puts a dent in one's car, the holiday hotel that does not come up to expectations, the landlord's failure to do routine repairs—one generally grins (or groans) and bears it oneself and on the whole probably expects others to do likewise. A society where everyone was actively engaged in asserting his or her legal rights might be an uncomfortable place. (It is relevant in that context that in nine out of ten legal problems with a money value in Genn's study, the amount involved was under £5,000.[28])

Trying for research purposes to evaluate someone else's decision to do nothing in pursuing a legal remedy is therefore an exercise fraught with difficulties. It is only in the rare extreme case that one can confidently assess the failure to act as problematic rather than understandable or even laudable.

Can anything be done to change people's appreciation of their legal situation and so influence their decision whether or not to take up the cudgels? I suspect that the scope for making a difference is not as great as is sometimes supposed. No doubt, more information about law, legal remedies, the legal system and about how to get advice, assistance and representation, would help—and it seems certain that in the coming years there will be an explosion in the amount of such information available, notably for instance, on the Internet. Nonetheless I would be very surprised if the information explosion greatly affects the basic shape of what I have called the pyramid. One reason is that millions of people are functionally illiterate and are therefore unlikely to be able to take advantage of personally having

---

[28] At p. 259.

access to information about legal problems and legal remedies.[29] More importantly, Professor Genn's study suggests that people generally fail to pursue their legal remedies for a variety of reasons other than a lack of relevant information or advice.

It is conventional wisdom that people would use the official legal system more if it were more user-friendly and cheaper. The Woolf reforms were essentially based on that thesis. The evidence, however, is to the contrary.

The history of the small claims court is in this respect instructive. When the county court was established in 1846 it had a maximum jurisdiction of £20. The jurisdiction gradually increased but relative to the High Court, the county court was the place for small claims. Yet those who used the system as plaintiffs were basically traders to recover debts. The Consumer Council's 1970 study, *Justice out of Reach*, showed that individuals hardly ever used the county court, as plaintiffs. That realisation led to the establishment in 1973 of the small claims court within the county court, with a special procedure designed to make it more attractive to ordinary people. A small claims case, typically, is handled in a private hearing in the judge's chambers, usually without lawyers. The parties are seated across the table from each other, with the district judge at its head. Neither the judge nor lawyers (if there are any) wear wigs or robes. The judge may help parties who appear without a lawyer to make their case. The atmosphere is likely to be considerably more relaxed and informal than proceedings in open court where the judge and the lawyers are wigged and robed and where the traditional adversary system operates. The general rule is that each side pays its own costs. The system is popular amongst those who use it. Professor John Baldwin's recent survey of the view of litigants in the county court concluded that whereas almost every interview with litigants who had been through the ordinary open court trial produced complaints, there were few complaints from the small claims litigants and that they broadly liked the system. ("No matter what criterion of litigant satisfaction was adopted, the small claims regime came out ahead—and by a wide margin."[30])

---

[29] A survey of 8,000 members of the public for whom English was their first language concluded that about 16 per cent of the adult population are functionally illiterate and that 8 million people are so bad at reading and writing that they cannot cope with the demands of modern life (*Adult Basic Skills*, Basic Skills Agency Survey (1998)).

[30] J. Baldwin, "Litigants' Experiences of Adjudication in the County Courts", [1999] 18 *Civil Justice Quarterly*, 12 at 39.

The small claims jurisdiction has been rapidly increased and now stands at £5,000.[31] Far more cases are handled in the small claims system than in ordinary hearings in the county court,[32] but if one asks the question who uses the small claims court, the answer is still, above all, small business to recover debts. Professor John Baldwin's verdict, on the basis of extensive research in this country, the United States and in Canada, was:

> "The evidence in this and other studies shows . . . that, while such mechanisms provide a means whereby access to justice might be extended, in practice they continue to be used by very limited sectors of the population, particularly professional people or those representing business interests. And any hopes that the small claims context might provide an avenue through which the poor might find redress for their grievances seem to have no empirical support whatever."[33]

In fact Baldwin's view is that recent increases in the jurisdiction have not even had the effect of bringing in new cases. Rather it seems to have resulted merely in transferring cases that would previously have been dealt with in the ordinary procedure to the small claims arena.[34] In itself that may be worthwhile but it is not the purpose of having small claims courts.

If the user friendly and relatively inexpensive small claims courts will not bring in the punters, there is obviously little hope that simplifying the procedure or reducing the costs in the *ordinary* courts will have that effect.

Is the answer therefore to try to encourage people to use some form of Alternative Dispute Resolution method? There is no doubt that there is today a powerful movement of informed opinion both in this country and in many other countries that

---

[31] The £75 limit was raised in 1975 to £200. In 1979 it went up to £500 and in 1991 to £1,000. Lord Woolf's Interim report proposed that it be increased to £3,000 save for personal injury cases and that was implemented in 1996. When the Woolf reforms were introduced in April 1999, the jurisdiction was raised to £5,000, save for personal injury and housing cases involving claims of over £1,000.

[32] In 1998 there were some 14,000 ordinary proceedings compared with some 98,500 small claims cases. (*Judicial Statistics*, Cm. 4371 (1998), Table 4.7, p. 40.)

[33] J. Baldwin, *Small Claims in the County Courts in England and Wales: The Bargain Basement of Civil Justice* (Clarendon, Oxford, 1997), p. 133.

[34] See J. Baldwin, "Increasing the small claims limit", *New Law Journal*, (February 27, 1998), pp. 274, 276.

favours ADR. It is, as they say, the flavour of the month. In his Interim Report, Lord Woolf devoted a whole chapter to the subject. His recommendations are reflected in the new Civil Procedure Rules.[35] One of the ways in which the courts are told to manage cases in the Overriding Objective stated in Rule 1 of the new rules is by encouraging the parties to use alternative dispute resolution procedure where that is appropriate.[36] Failure to co-operate with the court's suggestions regarding ADR can result in costs penalties.[37]

The legal profession, very sensibly, has already demonstrated great interest in adapting to this new development which shows signs of being a lucrative new form of business. It was, for instance, reported in October that the international law firm Baker & McKenzie currently valued its global arbitration cases at £6 billion.[38]

Allen & Overy's partner in charge of arbitration was quoted as saying that he personally was handling billions on a regular basis.[39] A consultant who is doing mediation full-time for Clifford Chance said it was the clients who were taking the lead. ("It is a very client-driven process because it puts clients in control of the outcome."[40]) ADR involving amounts of millions or billions will mainly be confined to a tiny elite of practitioners. But there are many signs that the general idea of ADR, be it mediation, arbitration, early neutral evaluation or whatever, is catching on amongst the professionals and there are more and more ADR providers of various kinds.[41]

Is it catching on amongst the potential customers?

Here one runs into an awkward fact. Although a Consumer Council survey in 1995 showed that a healthy majority of people said they would have preferred mediation or arbitration to a full trial, there is little sign that people actually offered the opportunity are inclined to take it. A recent study of the experimental scheme to promote ADR at the Central London County Court

---

[35] See especially CPR r. 26.4.
[36] CPR r. 1.4(2).
[37] See generally District Judge Trent, "ADR and the new Civil Procedure Rules", *New Law Journal*, (March 19, 1999), p. 410.
[38] *The Lawyer* (October 18, 1999), p. 7.
[39] *The Lawyer* (October 25, 1999), p. 12.
[40] *ibid.*
[41] For a valuable review of the developments and of the issues see M. Palmer and S. Roberts, *Dispute Processes: ADR and the Primary Forms of Decision Making* (Butterworths, 1998).

shows how far away we are from broad acceptance of the concept. All litigants involved in non-family civil disputes of over £3,000 were offered mediation at the nominal cost of £25. The study, again by Professor Hazel Genn, found that despite the very low cost, only five per cent of litigants approached took up the offer. Those who did use the service achieved a settlement in just under two-thirds (62 per cent) of cases and generally were satisfied. In those cases, the process promoted and speeded up settlement and reduced conflict. But it was unclear to what extent successful mediation saved costs—a critical question. Where it was unsuccessful, the mediation had the effect of increasing costs. The cost of the unsuccessful mediation had to be added to the cost of the traditional approach through the courts. Also the level of damages was distinctly lower than that of the courts.[42]

Mediation for would-be divorcing couples under the Family Law Act 1996 seems also to be moving extremely slowly. The 1996 Act provided that couples considering divorce would be required to attend an information meeting at which they would get information about marriage counselling and on mediation. Results from pilot studies of the provisions based on voluntary attendance at such meetings proved disappointing. The numbers electing to use mediation were very low. Only seven per cent of those who attended the information meetings went on to mediation.[43] The pilots were not in fact designed to test the extent to which information meetings would divert people into mediation though the Lord Chancellor seems to be using the results as his excuse for not going ahead with compulsory information meetings. Whatever the merits of this issue, however, it seems likely that only a small minority of divorcing couples will voluntarily opt for mediation. Quite apart from other reasons, it has to be borne in mind that for mediation to operate both partners must want it.

ADR is not some form of magic potion. The five-year Rand Corporation study of civil justice reforms, based on 10,000 cases

---

[42] H. Genn, *The Central London County Court Pilot Mediation Scheme*, LCD Research Series 5/98 (1998). See also N. Gould and M. Cohen, "ADR: Appropriate Dispute Resolution in the UK Construction Industry", *Civil Justice Quarterly* (April 1998), pp. 103–127. The conclusion was that although formalised mediation was only rarely invoked, it was a technique suitable for some cases.

[43] *Law Society's Gazette* (July 21, 1999), p. 22.

in federal courts in 16 States, looked also at ADR (mediation and early neutral evaluation) schemes. The report found no statistical evidence that these forms of ADR "significantly affected time to disposition or litigation costs".[44] I am wholly in favour of exploring the potential for every available method of ADR, but however much it expands, I do not believe that ADR will change the basic shape of the pyramid of disputes. Cases that get as far as starting legal proceedings represent the very top end of the pyramid of disputes. Those that are handled instead through some form of ADR are likely to be a small fraction of that number. My sense therefore is that ADR is unlikely to be more than a valuable but small side-show for the handling of some legal disputes.

Professor Hugh Collins, of the LSE Law Department, recently put his finger on the nub of the general point I am making when he wrote in regard to contractual disputes,

> "The contemporary emphasis of public policy to provide access to justice seems to be aimed at redistributing a 'good' that parties to contractual disputes do not want. Consumers probably do not want to be bothered by formal dispute processes . . . "[45].

I believe the same is more or less true right across the vast canvas of civil disputes, with the exception of matrimonial matters where legal proceedings are common.[46] When a dispute occurs, most people are prepared to complain and many are prepared to go so far as to take advice, but on the whole, for a great variety of understandable reasons, they show little interest in using any of the forms of civil justice.

I believe that this is not to be regarded as necessarily a bad thing. I also believe that to the extent that it is a bad thing, there is probably very little that can be done to change that situation.

Does that mean that we should give up attempts to improve the civil justice system? The answer, of course, is "No." We should do whatever we can to make it work as well as possible for those who choose to use it. The question then is what reforms *will* improve the system?

---

[44] For details regarding the Rand study see M. Zander, "How does judicial case management work?", *New Law Journal* (March 7, 1997), pp. 353–355.

[45] H. Collins, *op. cit.*, n. 9 above, p. 351.

[46] In cases concerning divorce and separation in Professor Genn's sample, 62 per cent involved legal proceedings (*op. cit.* n. 10 above, p. 150).

Civil Justice

Some changes seem perversely designed actually to make matters worse. That applies to the recent significant increase in court fees combined with the deplorable decision that the costs of running the civil courts, including even the costs of judicial salaries, should be recovered in full from litigants. The increase in fees has aroused widespread condemnation from all sides.[47] The policy of making the courts self-financing which was introduced by Lord Mackay[48] did not at the time provoke the uproar that might have been expected. But Sir Richard Scott, Vice Chancellor and Head of Civil Justice, was one who did speak up, describing the policy as "indefensible from a constitutional point of view". The civil justice system, with the criminal justice system and the police, he said, was one of the three pillars on which the structure of justice in a civilised community stood. No-one would suggest that the criminal justice system or the police should be self-financing. Why, Sir Richard said, should it be suggested of the civil justice system?

> "A policy which treats the civil justice system merely as a service to be offered at cost in the market place, and to be paid for by those who choose to use it, profoundly and dangerously mistakes the nature of the system and its constitutional function".[49]

He expressed the hope that the then new Labour Government would consign the policy of making the civil justice system self-financing to the dustbin. Instead, Lord Irvine continued the policy, ratcheting up the fees even higher and adding the new ingredient that the farther the case goes, the higher the fees. There is probably now no hope that this highly objectionable policy will be reversed.

In April of this year, the civil justice system underwent the most radical reform of the century through the implementation of the Woolf reform package. Lord Woolf's proposals were welcomed by almost everyone. I was one of the few who did

---

[47] The £80 fee payable on allocation of cases to their appropriate track has aroused particular ire. In January 2000 it was announced that it would be abolished for claims under £1000, but a Consultation Paper in February proposed further increases in fees—see *Law Society's Gazette* (February 3, 2000), p. 1.

[48] In 1988/1989 the Conservative Government adopted the policy that the civil justice system should be self-financing. In 1991 it decided that this should include judicial salaries.

[49] Transcript of a speech to the County Court Advisers' Group, May 16, 1997.

not welcome them, fearing that they would on balance make matters worse rather than better.[50] It will take a while before one can judge whether those fears were justified. The first indications suggest that the new procedural rules are bedding in well and there seems to be a general feeling that they have got off to a good start, but these early and somewhat encouraging signs do not throw much light on the overall impact of the reforms.

Before explaining why I continue to have my doubts, I want to pay tribute to Lord Woolf for the remarkable achievement of getting his project off the drawing board and into operation, and within so short a time. It can truly be said that he had a vision and that he largely translated it into action. The essence of the vision was that the well-known ills of civil litigation were mainly the result of the system and of the ways that lawyers abused it. Litigation was conducted in too adversary a manner. Delays were endemic because a leisurely pace was accepted and no attention was paid to time-limits. Costs were out of proportion to the amount at stake.

Lord Woolf's answer was nothing less than to change the culture—to transfer the management of cases from the lawyers to the courts, to make everyone adhere to time-tables, to require early preparation of cases and to penalise unreasonable conduct by the parties. The new rules start with the Overriding Objective that cases should be dealt with justly. This is defined to mean ensuring, so far as practicable, that parties be on an equal footing; that a case be dealt with in ways that are proportionate to the amount of money involved, to the importance of the case, to its complexity and to the financial position of each party; ensuring that it is dealt with expeditiously and fairly; and allotting to it an appropriate share of the court's resources, while taking into account the need to allot resources to other cases.[51]

A consultation paper recently issued by the Lord Chancellor's Department on plans for the Evaluation of the Civil Justice Reforms said that, broadly, the aim of the reforms had been described as seeking to reduce delay, cost and complexity and

---

[50] See especially, M. Zander, "The Woolf Report: Forwards or Backwards for the new Lord Chancellor?", *Civil Justice Quarterly*, (July 1997), pp. 208–227. For Lord Woolf's response see "Medics, Lawyers and the Courts", *Civil Justice Quarterly* (October 1997), pp. 302–317. For the writer's reply see *New Law Journal* (May 23, 1997), p. 768.

[51] CPR r. 1.1.

to increase fairness and certainty for litigants. That, it said, provided five indicators against which success could be judged.

The single most important element of the Woolf reforms I suppose was to reduce the costs of litigation. One of my chief reasons for opposing the reforms was my belief that they will instead raise costs. The main reason is that the new rules require or encourage the parties to do more work earlier than before. The front-loading of costs bites on most cases—those that settle as much as those that go all the way to trial. It affects even cases where no legal proceedings are ever started. Almost all claims settle, usually without any form of legal proceedings. (A leading insurance company has told me that in the 12 months to October 1999 it closed 16,500 personal injury cases. Nearly nine out of ten (87 per cent) settled without any legal proceedings being started. In 12 per cent the case settled after proceedings had started and 1 per cent reached trial.) A feature of the new system is the Pre-action Protocols which set out what is now to be regarded as proper conduct by the parties in regard to such matters as early disclosure of information before an action has even started. The Personal Injury Protocol runs to 17 pages; the Protocol on Medical Negligence Claims runs to 25 pages. The purpose of the protocols is to create a climate or environment of reasonable behaviour by both sides. Failure to comply with the protocols can be taken into account by the court at the end of the case when it comes to allocate costs. Under the protocols the parties are required to do a variety of things before starting proceedings that previously they would not necessarily have done at that stage, if at all. To the extent that cases would previously have settled without such work, the costs incurred as a result of the protocols will be greater than before. The same applies to work done earlier in response to the requirement that each side put its case from the outset. Moreover, the new emphasis on moving things along according to a tight timetable will cause both sides to do more preparation before commencing proceedings instead of leaving it, as before, to a later stage. One might say, "Quite right too. The sooner the litigants get their tackle in order the better." However, the effect is to front-load costs unnecessarily if the case would have settled without it. It is possible that in some of those cases the settlement will come earlier or be more soundly based by virtue of more information. But that is mere speculation. What seems clear is that the introduction of the Woolf reforms will cause a general, across-the-board raising of costs through the direct and indirect effects of case management.

The greater hands-on case management for Multi-track cases (those involving amounts of over £15,000), with two pre-trial hearings, will generate even greater additional costs. Lord Woolf's hope is that such additional expenditure pre-trial will save significant costs at the trial, but there is no empirical evidence to support that, whilst there are studies that show that pre-trial hearings do not shorten trials.[52]

Whilst judicial case management may result in better preparation of cases for trial, it is a recipe for increased rather than decreased costs[53] as Lord Woolf finally acknowledged in 1997, a year after publication of his Final Report.[54] It is interesting to speculate what impact his recommendations would have had if this admission had been made much earlier.

The Lord Chancellor's Department's paper on evaluating the Woolf reforms suggests that the hoped-for advance in regard to fairness will flow, for instance, from the impact of sanctions for unreasonable behaviour and from the new rules on claimants' offers to settle.

I am wholly in favour of the new procedure for claimants' offers to settle. The defendant, typically an insurance company,

---

[52] See especially the study of matched samples in 3,000 personal injury cases in New Jersey which found that pre-trial conferences lowered rather than raised the efficiency of the system by absorbing a great deal of court time without any compensating savings. M. Rosenberg, *The Pre-trial Conference and Effective Justice*, (Columbia University Press, 1964), p. 68. There are two studies of criminal cases that have come to the same conclusion: M. Levi, *The Investigation, Prosecution and Trial of Serious Fraud*, Royal Commission on Criminal Justice (Research Study No. 14, 1993), p. 105 ("None of the defence lawyers I interviewed argued the pre-trial reviews had any significant effect on the development of the case"); M. Zander and P. Henderson, *The Crown Court Study*, Royal Commission on Criminal Justice (Research Study No. 19, 1993), s. 2.8.9. (Crown court judges were asked whether the pre-trial review had saved much time or money at trial. Two-thirds said no, a quarter said a little and 8 per cent said a fair amount of time had been saved. Only 1 per cent said a great deal of time had been saved.)

[53] This was one of the most important findings of the major study of the impact of judicial case management by the Institute of Civil Justice of the Rand Corporation. For details see M. Zander, "How does judicial case management work?", *New Law Journal* (March 7, 1997), p. 353 and April 11, 1997, p. 539.

[54] "While I favour the greater case management which is now possible I recognise that case management does involve the parties in more expense . . ." (Lord Woolf, "Medics, Lawyers and the Courts", *Civil Justice Quarterly* (October 1997), pp. 302, 314.)

Civil Justice

has always had the right to pay a sum of money into court as an offer of settlement. If the plaintiff chooses to reject the offer and then fails to beat the sum paid-in, he is penalised severely in costs. For him it is a form of Russian roulette, with a devastating impact if he and his advisers guess wrongly as to what damages the court will award. Now the claimant can put the insurance company under some, though hardly the equivalent, pressure. That is a gain in terms of fairness and I believe that it will also result in more early settlements.

But the application of sanctions under the new rules is a very different matter. Sanctions are central to the Woolf project. In his Interim and Final Reports, Lord Woolf was insistent that there had to be a sea-change of culture in regard to time-limits. The rules of court "were being flouted on a vast scale". Timetables were not adhered to and other orders were not complied with if it did not suit the parties to do so. There had been overwhelming support from all sides "for effective, appropriate and fair sanctions".[55] The effectiveness of sanctions would require a much tougher approach from the judges (he said, "There is no doubt that some judges at first instance, especially Masters and District Judges, will need to develop a more robust approach to the task of managing cases and ensuring that their orders are not flouted."[56]), and the judges would need to be supported by the appellate courts. ("Procedural decisions must not be overturned lightly ... This is not simply a matter of limiting appeals. It goes to a change of culture ... "[57]).

My concern is that this policy does not allow sufficiently for ordinary human frailty, for the difficulties of running a busy lawyer's office, or for the fact that the cause of delay will often be wholly outside the control of the lawyers being penalised by the court. (A 1994 study of delay in the High Court and the county courts by KPMG Peat Marwick identified a variety of reasons for delay. The two that it said gave rise to the most significant delay were inexperience or inefficiency in the handling of cases by the parties' solicitors and time taken to get medical or other reports.[58])

To make compliance with the rules central to the system of civil justice is to give procedural rules an importance they do

[55] Final Report, p. 72, paras. 1, 2.
[56] *ibid.*, p. 76, para. 15.
[57] *ibid.*, p. 76, para. 15.
[58] *Study of Causes of Delay in the High Court and the county courts* (LCD, 1994).

not deserve. The point was made by Sir Jack Jacob Q.C., the leading civil proceduralist of our time, in his Dissent to the Report of the Winn Committee in 1968:

> "The admonition by Lord Justice Bowen that 'courts do not exist for the sake of discipline' should be reflected in the principle that rules of court should not be framed on the basis of imposing penalties or producing automatic consequences for non-compliance with the rules or orders of the court. The function of rules of court is to provide guide-lines not trip wires and they fulfil their function most where they intrude least in the course of litigation."[59]

When the court visits severe penalties for a breach of the rules it is generally acting harshly in the particular case *pour encourager les autres*. It is predictable that sometimes the judges will take this approach—hardening their hearts and administering the punishment in the name of the principle that the rules must not be flouted. (Incidentally, when they do so, lay litigants will often find themselves penalised for the failures of their lawyers, not an obvious advance in justice.) Sometimes, however, the court will be persuaded by the excuses and justifications put forward on behalf of the party in default.[60] What is predictable is that the courts will not be consistent in their approach which is a recipe for unequal justice, or less fairness.

The problem of inconsistency of approach by the judges creating unfairness applies equally to a whole raft of new discretions given to the judges by the new rules. Under Lord Woolf's judicial case management, the judge who is managing the case knows only what is presented to him by the parties. He has to make snap decisions based often on inadequate information. Inevitably, through no fault of his, he will sometimes make decisions that are unwise or inappropriate. But it will be difficult to appeal such discretionary decisions since the appeal courts, understandably, will not want to second-guess the

---

[59] *Report of the Committee on Personal Injury Litigation*, Cmnd. 369 (1968), pp. 151–152.
[60] In *Biguzzi v. Rank Leisure plc* [1999] 4 All E.R. 934 the Court of Appeal *per* Lord Woolf confirmed: (1) that time-limits were important and had to be enforced by the courts; (2) that the courts had an unfettered discretion to strike out cases where there had been a failure to comply with a rule; but that (3) the court might instead use other powers to make it clear that delays would not be tolerated. ("In a great many situations those other powers will be the appropriate ones to adopt because they produce a more just result" (at 940)).

procedural judge. As Lord Woolf said in his Final Report, "management decisions are pre-eminently matters of discretion with which an appeal court would seldom interfere".[61] So the move to judicial case management not only greatly increases the risk of inappropriate decisions resulting from the judge's lack of familiarity with the case, but equally increases the volume of low-level, inconsistent discretionary decisions that are in practice unappealable. That again seems to me a step backward for fairness.

Inconsistency of approach by the judges is a serious problem in the small claims courts. And the vast increase in the jurisdiction of these courts correspondingly increases the impact of the problem. The problem of variation in how the judges conduct small claims cases has been highlighted by Professor John Baldwin's research. The difference is not just a matter of style. It affects the extent to which the judge is prepared to help the parties to produce evidence or to act as his own expert when no relevant evidence is proffered by either side.[62] It applies equally to whether the judge feels constrained to apply the law. Baldwin reports that only a minority of the 33 district judges he interviewed thought it was their duty strictly to apply the law. The majority said they thought they were entitled to disregard the law if in their view strictly applying it would produce injustice.[63] This is strong meat. In his Interim Report, Lord Woolf said "it is questionable whether such differences are acceptable even in a jurisdiction limited to £1,000" and that any inclination to follow common sense rather than the principles of law should be resisted in the interests of consistency.[64] Baldwin, following the same line of thinking, observed,

> "Decision making can easily become inconsistent, capricious, uncertain, even biased, and in the process, the substantive legal rights of individuals may be undermined. Moreover, while flexibility is doubtless desirable in dealing with small claims, it can create uncertainty for lay litigants and their advisers."[65]

---

[61] Final Report, p. 154, para. 5. See to like effect *Biguzzi v. Rank Leisure plc* [1999] 4 All E.R. 934 at 941, CA.
[62] Baldwin reports that in 91 of the 109 small claims cases observed, no witnesses at all attended: ("Small Claims Hearings: the 'Interventionist' Role Played by District Judges", *Civil Justice Quarterly* (January 1998), pp. 20, 28.
[63] *ibid.*, p. 29.
[64] *Access to Justice*, Interim Report, (1995), p. 109.
[65] *op. cit.*, n. 62 above, at p. 31.

Lord Woolf thought that the answer was more guidance and training for district judges in playing the interventionist role to achieve greater consistency.[66] I regard that as unrealistic. The differences flow from different perceptions of how to be a judge. Such differences cannot be smoothed away by training or guidance. Especially they cannot be smoothed away in the context of low-level decisions in private hearings often with no lawyers present and where appeals are rare. Inconsistency of approach by the judges in the small claims jurisdiction is inevitable.[67] I am not sure that it is acceptable in cases involving amounts of up to £5,000. I would certainly question whether it is acceptable in cases involving larger amounts.

One of the important new rules introduced as part of the Woolf reforms gives the judge at the end of the case the task of allocating costs in accordance with which party has won on the different issues raised and in accordance with his view as to how reasonably or unreasonably the parties have conducted themselves both during the trial and pre-trial—including even before the proceedings were started.[68] This replaces the previous rule applied by the courts under which the winner more or less automatically got his costs. The issue required no argument; the decision took less than a minute. Clearly the aim of the new approach is to increase the fairness of the costs system. One effect will be to increase costs since time will now have to be taken—sometimes at a separate later hearing—to delve into the rights and wrongs of the conduct of the case by the respective parties. Also the costs decision, though aimed to increase justice, may do the exact opposite if the judge makes his decision on the basis of an insufficient grasp of the facts. In an early landmark decision interpreting these new rules the High Court judge reduced the winning local authority's costs from 100 per cent to 75 per cent on account of relative success on the issues, and then to 50 per cent on account of conduct. The solicitor for the winner, writing about the case, made the following understandably critical observations:

[66] Interim Report, pp. 108–10; Final Report, p. 98.
[67] Research on small claims in Canada found similarly that judges varied greatly in their approach, from the strict legalists to those who seek rather to do justice: R.A. Macdonald, "Judicial Scripts in the Dramaturgy of the Small Claims Court", *Canadian Journal of Law and Society* (1996, Vol. 11), p. 63. See also M. Zander, "Consistency in the exercise of discretionary powers", *New Law Journal*, November 1, 1996, p. 1590.
[68] CPR, r. 44.3(4), (5).

Civil Justice

"The decision to reduce the apportionment which the judge would otherwise have made in the council's favour from 75 per cent to 50 per cent as a result of the council's conduct is a subjective and wholly imprecise assessment by the judge of the way in which he considered the conduct of the litigation had increased the costs. The judge had only the information which had been made available during the trial upon which to make this assessment and no specific evidence was put forward by either party on costs . . . [T]here was no information upon which any sort of reasoned decision could be made as to the amount of such reduction."[69]

That goes to the question of whether the judge's allocation of costs is likely to be just. There is also the effect of increased uncertainty about the outcome and its potential impact on the attractiveness of using the legal system at all. The points on which the winner in that case had failed, which led the judge to reduce the costs order to 75 per cent, had been decided at trial only after lengthy oral evidence for and against. They were not spurious points. If the winner is not going to get his costs for costs incurred on issues on which he lost, how are lawyers supposed to advise their clients as to what points to take? Are they to advise that reasonable and seemingly winnable points should not be taken for fear that they might be lost? The new rule introduces a range of new uncertainties.

As to increasing certainty and reducing delay, the new system should secure some gains. To know from an early stage that the hearing will be on a particular day or during a particular week and that it is difficult to get the court to grant an extension of the timetable no doubt helps to concentrate minds and to move things along. Not that it necessarily follows that things have actually speeded up. As has been seen, one of the effects may simply be that the case is prepared before proceedings are launched onto the Fast Track conveyor belt. But even if it is handled more quickly there may be a price to be paid for the increase in certainty and tighter timetables. The point is clearest in the Fast Track, which will apply to most cases involving amounts of between £5,000 and £15,000. All cases in the Fast Track must be given a date of trial, failing which a window of two or three weeks, not more than 30 weeks from the date of allocation. If a case is too complex to be prepared in 30 weeks it

---

[69] P. Thomas, "The new costs regime under the CPR", *Solicitors' Journal* (October 8, 1999), pp. 926, 928.

should be allocated to the Multi-track. But how can the judge allocating the case be expected reliably to get the allocation decision right? There will be cases, perhaps many cases, in which it turns out that 30 weeks is not enough time. The refusal to grant an extension of time in such a case[70] will undeniably give increased certainty to the system, but if there is not enough time to prepare the case it may cause injustice to one party or perhaps to both.

Reactions after six or so months of the Woolf reforms have been mixed. A preliminary survey published by the Law Society in September 1999 stated:

> "The majority of respondents believe that although it is early days, the Civil Procedure Rules are working quite well. However there is a feeling that the real test will come when Fast Track cases start coming up for trial. Some practitioners have reported that backlogs at county courts are causing a large problem and that interpretation of the rules appears to vary from court to court. There is also concern that in some cases the new rules appear to have increased costs and not reduced them. ('For example, some solicitors are having to spend their week travelling around the country to attend case management conferences.') Also some respondents complained that costing files at the case management conference stage in the manner of a summary assessment involves detailed work which does not progress matters in any way."[71]

On the matter of single experts, it seems that, at least in Fast Track cases, parties are opting to have a single expert for both sides more frequently than had been expected.[72]

Thompson's, the country's largest personal injury law firm with 17 offices nationwide, which at any one time is handling

---

[70] The rules state that where there has been a failure to comply with directions, an application to vacate the trial date will only be granted in exceptional circumstances (CPR PD28, para. 5.4(1)–(3)). See further *Law Society's Gazette* (November 3, 1999), p. 46.

[71] Law Society, *Responses to Woolf Network Questionnaire No. 1* (September 1999). The survey was based on the responses of 18 out of 31 "Woolf Co-ordinators", experienced solicitors from firms in different parts of the country. They were asked to fill out the questionnaire after speaking to people in their own firms and to others.

[72] In a survey of experts carried out six months after the introduction of the Woolf reforms, nearly half (45 per cent) had already had experience of being the single agreed expert in a case. See *Law Society's Gazette* (November 3, 1999), p. 3.

thousands of personal injury cases, recently[73] sent the LCD a short memorandum indicating its first views as to how the reforms were working. Its verdict was mixed. The Fast Track, it said, was working in the sense of producing settlements. The new rule permitting the claimant to make an offer of settlement was also working and increasing settlements. Pre-action protocols, however, did not seem to be leading to early settlements. On judicial case management, the centrepiece of the Woolf reforms, the memorandum was scathing:

> "Judicial case management is in our experience a disaster. It is involving far greater work than before and that means far greater cost. It is leading to the front-loading of case work. The judiciary are applying sanctions without having considered first what the case is about and what is happening within it."

The Lord Chancellor's Department plans itself to conduct and to commission others to conduct research on the effects of the Woolf reforms. The question is not whether the new system has positive features. I have no doubt that it does. The question is whether the strengths of the new system outweigh the weaknesses as compared with the balance of strengths and weaknesses in the old system. It will be a considerable time before we can begin to reach a concluded view and in all probability even then there will be disagreement.

Whatever the ultimate verdict on these major reforms, there will be need for further improvements. The task of providing a good system for those who come seeking civil justice is permanent. We should be ready to return to the drawing board again and again and yet again.

But whilst tinkering with the system we should bear in mind that we are operating at the very top of the pyramid and that the overwhelming majority of disputes will always be dealt with and resolved (or not resolved) without recourse to any form of dispute resolution system be it mainstream courts or some form of ADR.

We should also bear in mind that it is difficult to be sure whether that is a matter for concern or for celebration. Is it a good thing or a bad thing when someone goes in pursuit of civil justice? It could be either or even both at the same time. One

[73] October 4, 1999.

would not wish a lawsuit on anyone, yet taking up the cudgels is often the only way to get or to preserve one's rights. Does one want more of it or less of it? I find myself unable to answer that question.

3. Criminal Justice

Criminal justice encompasses a vast ramshackle system (if system is the word) involving a great variety of institutions and professions. They include the police, the Crown Prosecution Service, barristers and solicitors in private practice, courts, judges and magistrates, the probation service, the prisons and a variety of other penal establishments. Public expenditure on criminal justice currently runs at some £12 billion annually.[1]

Not that all this does much to deal with the problem of crime. According to official Home Office figures for crimes against individuals and their property, of 100 offences committed, only 45 get reported to the police, 24 are recorded by the police, five are cleared up by the police, and just two result in a conviction.[2]

So the criminal courts touch only the fringes of the problem of crime. Perhaps this is less surprising when one considers that there is no basis for a sentencer to believe that he or she knows what sentence will work in terms of reducing recidivism. Statistics show that a depressingly high proportion of defendants are reconvicted within a couple of years or so of completing their sentence, regardless of the sentence.[3] Custodial penalty or non-custodial penalty, statistically it seems to make little difference.[4] Some offenders cease offending, or at least they are not reconvicted, which is not necessarily quite the same. Thus a court that passes sentence has no sound basis for predicting how the sentence it imposes will affect the individual defendant.

---

[1] Digest 4, *Information on the criminal justice system in England and Wales*, Home Office, (1999) p. 69. In 1993/1994 it was £9.4 billion (Digest 3, *ibid.*, p. 68).
[2] *ibid.*, pp. 27, 29.
[3] For those commencing community penalties or discharged from prison in 1994, about 70 per cent of offenders under 21 were reconvicted within two years. For those between 21–24 it was 62 per cent, for those between 25 to 29 it was 52 per cent and for those aged 30 or over it was 38 per cent (*ibid.*, 1999, p. 61).
[4] *ibid.*, p. 60.

However, the problem of how to make an impact on the problem of crime is not my subject. I am concerned here rather with how the system functions after a suspect has been apprehended up to the final disposition of an appeal and post-appeal remedies. This was broadly the range of topics addressed by the Runciman Royal Commission on Criminal Justice which reported in 1993.[5]

The Royal Commission was set up in 1991 at a moment of widespread concern about the system after a series of spectacular miscarriage of justice cases. There may therefore have been an expectation that the Commission would come forward with radical proposals for reform, but that did not happen. The Commission unanimously concluded that the system was basically sound and that what was needed was not radical change but rather a general tuning-up of most of the existing working parts of the system. Given the sense of crisis at the time of the setting up of the Commission, it was very striking how little call there was for significant change. In the 600 or so memoranda of evidence submitted to the Commission there were, for instance, virtually none that urged the adoption of the continental so-called inquisitorial approach under which the judges rather than the parties play the dominant role both pre-trial and at trial. Virtually no one proposed changes in the familiar basic institutions: the police with responsibility for laying charges; the Crown Prosecution Service responsible for deciding whether the case goes forward and, if so, on what charges; summary trial by benches of three lay magistrates supplemented in some urban courts by a small number of professional stipendiaries who sit alone; and trial of more serious cases in the Crown Court by judge and jury. There seemed equally to be general agreement that, despite a great deal of controversy at the time of its enactment, the 1984 Police and Criminal Evidence Act (PACE) had settled in well, and five years later merely needed some relatively minor adjustment.

Where virtually no one is urging radical reform it would be remarkable if a Royal Commission, with its balanced composition almost by definition a vehicle designed for compromise and moderation, were to recommend any dramatic changes. So it was hardly surprising that the Runciman Commission accepted these basic features of the existing system as given.

[5] The writer was a member of the Runciman Royal Commission.

In my first lecture I suggested that evaluation of the working parts of the criminal justice system requires consideration, in respect of each topic, of the appropriate balance between the interests of the prosecution, the interests of the defence and the interests of due economy and efficiency. Obviously in a single lecture on criminal justice one cannot cover all the relevant topics.

I start with an issue that was not addressed by the Runciman Royal Commission—the question of the difference between justice in the Crown Court and justice in the magistrates' court. Everyone would agree that they are different. Most would agree that the Crown Court is the superior model, which is why it deals with the most serious cases. But it does not follow that there is anything wrong with justice in the magistrates' court, which deals with well over 90 per cent of all cases.

The James Committee[6] in 1975 said that the widespread belief that trial by jury was superior to trial by magistrates seemed to be based on two main grounds. One was that a randomly selected jury brought a more impartial mind to bear on the issues than can magistrates "who inevitably become 'case hardened' and may be too ready to accept the prosecution case".[7] The second was that jury trial was presided over by a professional judge, that both sides were generally represented by specialists in advocacy, that the pace was slower, resulting in the issues being brought out more thoroughly than was possible in a busy magistrates court with a crowded list.[8] The James Committee said there was very little information on which to compare the quality of justice dispensed by the two levels of courts.[9]

The Committee rejected the view that the higher acquittal rate in the Crown Court proved anything: "For it to be meaningful, it would be necessary to establish whether it was due to juries acquitting those who were in fact 'guilty' or magistrates' courts convicting 'the innocent' ".[10]

For all one knows, the difference in the acquittal rate may be the result of a very different approach to what is meant by the

---

[6] *The Distribution of Criminal Business between the Crown Court and Magistrates' Courts*, Cmnd. 6323 (1175).
[7] *ibid.*, at p. 18, para. 36.
[8] *ibid.*
[9] *ibid.*, at p. 18, para. 37.
[10] *ibid.*, at p. 19, para. 37.

Criminal Justice

requirement of proof beyond a reasonable doubt. A recent study on how ordinary citizens interpret the standard formula for the criminal standard of proof ("you must be satisfied so that you feel sure") showed that nearly three-quarters of the sample thought it meant "you must be 100% certain".[11] If that really is a widespread view it would go a long way to explain the fact that juries have a higher acquittal rate. It would also suggest that the formula should be changed.

The James Committee equally rejected the view that the very small number of appeals from the decisions of magistrates indicated general satisfaction with summary trial. ("There are many reasons why a convicted person may choose or feel compelled not to exercise his right of appeal although he genuinely believes that the conviction or sentence is unjust".[12]) The Committee declined to express a view as to the quality of justice dispensed by the two levels of court.

The Runciman Royal Commission recommended that proper research in the jury room should be permitted, but it seems unlikely that that proposal will be implemented.[13] The prospects of an empirical study being undertaken to compare decision-making by juries and magistrates is even more remote.

The James Committee referred to various improvements in summary jurisdiction, especially in regard to training of magistrates and court staff and in the expansion of legal aid, and said that continuing developments of that kind would "we hope go at least some way to removing what may appear to many defendants to be the unsatisfactory features of summary trial".[14] Developments of that kind have continued and are continuing. There have, for instance, been important recent changes in the

---

[11] J.W. Montgomery, "The criminal standard of proof", *New Law Journal* (April 24, 1998), pp. 582, 584. For further suggestions as to the reasons for the difference in the acquittal rate see, for instance, P. Darbyshire, "For the new Lord Chancellor—some causes for concern about magistrates" [1997] Crim. L.R. 861 at 870–872.

[12] *op. cit.*, n. 6 above, at p. 19, para. 38.

[13] *Report of the Royal Commission on Criminal Justice*, Cm. 2264 (1993), p. 2, para. 8. The Conservative Government in its Interim Response to the Royal Commission's Report (1994) indicated that it was "sympathetic" to the recommendation but that it was still considering the precise scope of such research. Even if the deliberations of the jury could be recorded for research purposes it does not follow that the same would be the case for the deliberations of the lay magistrates.

[14] *op. cit.*, n. 6 above, at p. 20, para. 40.

system for training lay magistrates. As from 1998 the training includes such topics as reaching impartial decisions (for example, raising awareness of one's own conditioning and personal prejudices, labelling and stereotyping, language and cultural differences and body language); and effective participation on the bench (for example, ensuring equality of treatment to all court users, ensuring that witnesses are not bullied, observing people and conduct, challenging discriminatory views). New magistrates are now assigned to experienced magistrates who act as mentors.

In 1998, the Lord Chancellor's Department ("LCD") issued a Consultation Paper regarding improving the qualifications of court clerks.[15] Also in 1998, the LCD issued a Consultation Paper on selection of magistrates. It raised for consideration whether the long-standing attempt to achieve a political balance on the magistrates' bench should be scrapped in favour of a new system that would attempt to achieve a balanced and more representative bench on the basis of a broader range of geo-economic factors.[16] However, it was announced in October that the Lord Chancellor had reluctantly decided to retain the "political balance" system for the time being as the proposed new geo-demographic system had failed to win sufficient support. The announcement stated that officials would be asked to try to develop a new approach looking at occupational categories, together with such factors as age, sex, and regional spread.[17]

These are all indications of a concern regarding at least the appearance of justice. But knowing how to improve the *quality* of justice is much more difficult. Research suggests, for instance, that sentencing disparities as between different magistrates' courts are not explained by the social class composition of the magistrates' bench.[18] If that is right, it follows that altering the

---

[15] "The Professional Qualification of Court Clerks in Magistrates' Courts", LCD (July 1998).
[16] "Political Balance in the Lay Magistracy", LCD (October 1998).
[17] LCD Press Notice, No. 329/99 (October 25, 1999). See also *Solicitors' Journal* (October 29, 1999), p. 992.
[18] See for instance, H. Mannheim *et al.*, "Magisterial policy in the London Juvenile Courts", *British Journal of Delinquency* (1957, Vol. 8), pp. 13–33, 119–138. No associations were found to exist between the sentencing practices of different courts and various possible sociological factors. The authors concluded that "the subjective or intuitive assessment of individual cases does

social class composition of the bench, whatever it may do for the reputation of the system, will not iron out such disparities.

The Lord Chancellor has recently caused upset in some quarters with the announcement that there is to be a research project to examine whether the current balance between the use of the 30,000 lay magistrates and the 100 or so full-time professional stipendiary magistrates is "correct", whether each is deployed in the most effective way and the weight of the argument for and against each. Some fear that this could be a signal that the lay magistracy is about to be consigned to the dust-heap. I regard that as most unlikely. The terms of reference for the inquiry specifically state, "The Government is committed to the principle of the lay magistracy continuing to play a significant part in our system of justice. Also the Government's overriding concern is to have in place a system of criminal justice in which the public have confidence." Even if it turns out that stipendiaries are actually cheaper than lay magistrates because of their much greater through-put of cases, I hope that this categorical statement of Government policy stands. The lay magistracy has its faults, but I would prefer most summary cases to be decided by three lay persons than by one professional, if only because three heads are better than one. In that context it is relevant that research in London by Professor Shari Diamond suggests that lay magistrates are slightly more lenient in sentencing than their professional colleagues.[19] Professor Diamond concluded that the difference was not the result of naiveté on the part of the lay magistrates:

> "a primary source of the lay magistrate's greater leniency appears to be the voluntary part-time role the magistrates play in the London courts. For the professional magistrate who sees general crime control as a major responsibility, the offender is only one element in the sentencing decision. In contrast, the lay magistrate is less concerned with the general sentencing policy of the court and focuses more on the individual offender than on the community at large."

in the main prevail" (pp. 13, 119). In a study of motoring cases Professor Roger Hood found that disparities in sentencing were not explicable simply in terms of differences in the personal backgrounds of justices. Rather he suggested that the best explanation was the philosophy of the particular bench to which they belonged. See R. Hood, *Sentencing the Motoring Offender* (Heinemann, 1972), p. 140.

[19] Shari S. Diamond, "Revising Images of Public Punitiveness: Sentencing by Lay and Professional English Magistrates", *Law and Social Inquiry* (1990, Vol. 15), pp. 191–221.

For me that is a powerful argument in favour of the lay magistracy.

No matter what reforms and improvements are made in regard to magistrates' courts, it is obvious that the main differences between the two levels of criminal court will remain.[20] They are systemic differences that flow from the essential nature of the two institutions. Since it seems to be accepted as a given by almost everyone, it is perhaps not sensible to treat it as a problem.

What definitely is a problem is the method of allocating cases to the two levels of court which has been and remains a subject of fierce controversy. Of all the 352 recommendations made by the Runciman Royal Commission, the one that provoked most controversy was that defendants should lose their right to insist on jury trial in what are called "either way" cases, and that if prosecution and defence could not agree, the mode of trial should be decided by the magistrates in the light of statutory criteria. The proposal was denounced by a wide variety of commentators for taking away a valuable (or rather, an invaluable) and historic right.[21]

Six years on, the Home Secretary, Mr Jack Straw announced this May that he intended to implement the proposal—despite having strongly criticised it when he was in opposition—and the bill to give effect to that intention has now been published.[22] The Government estimate that some 12,000 cases currently dealt with in the Crown Court would, as a result, be handled instead in the magistrates' court with a net saving in cost of some £105 million.[23]

The Runciman Commission was unanimous on the subject and I can report that its members, though bloodied, were unbowed by the storm of criticism that the proposal provoked. I acknowledge that reducing access to jury trial has the wrong ring to it. But there are powerful reasons that support this

---

[20] For an itemisation of the disadvantages of summary trial see N. Ley, "Inferior justice", *New Law Journal* (September 10, 1999), p. 1316.

[21] The defendant's right to elect does not date back to Magna Carta as some assert but rather to the Criminal Justice Act 1855 when the magistrates were given jurisdiction to try simple larceny cases involving five shillings or less *with the consent of the defendant*. That was the first time the defendant was given a power to choose.

[22] Criminal Justice (Mode of Trial) Bill, introduced in the House of Lords on November 18, 1999.

[23] Explanatory Notes to the Bill.

Criminal Justice

change. One is that a majority[24] of defendants who elect jury trial in either way cases later decide to plead guilty, often at the door of the Crown Court when the case has been prepared and listed as a contested case. The result is the waste of the time and effort of preparation of those cases not only for lawyers and police officers but also for victims and other lay witnesses.

Understandably, many defendants who elect Crown Court trial do so because of the higher acquittal rate. In a Home Office 1992 study, this was the most frequently mentioned reason for choosing the Crown Court by both defendants and solicitors.[25] In the view of the Royal Commission the defendant should no more have the right to choose the court that gives him a better chance of an acquittal than to choose a lenient judge. Another important factor, in the Commission's view, was that the same research showed that when samples were matched, judges were three times more likely to impose immediate custody, and sentences were on average two-and-a-half times as long.[26] Also, of course, cases dealt with in the Crown Court are hugely more expensive than those dealt with in the magistrates' courts.[27]

All of these were important, but I think that for most members of the Royal Commission the main reason was one of principle—that where prosecution and defence could not agree, it was for the system rather than the defendant to determine where he should be tried. The 1997 Narey *Review of Delay in the Criminal Justice System*[28] pushed this point of principle to its logical conclusion by recommending that the court should *always* determine the matter and this view has prevailed in the Government's bill. I see the force of that and do not object to it.

The statute will require the court to take into account all relevant matters, including the effect of a conviction on the

---

[24] There is dispute as to the proportion but there is no dispute that it is considerable. The latest estimate is that it is around 60 per cent—information supplied by the Home Office (February 2000).

[25] C. Hedderman and D. Moxon, *Magistrates' Court or Crown Court? Mode of Trial Decisions* (Home Office Research Study No. 125, HMSO, 1992), p. 20.

[26] *ibid.*, p. vii and Chap. 4.

[27] The Home Office estimated the cost of a substantive court proceeding excluding sentence in 1997/1998 at £550 in the magistrates' court and £8,600 in the Crown Court. The estimated cost of a sentence was £250 in the magistrates' court and £23,900 in the Crown Court. (*Digest 4, Information on the criminal justice system in England and Wales* (Home Office, October 1999), p. 73.)

[28] Chap. 6. Mr Martin Narey, who conducted the review, was a senior Home Office official.

defendant's livelihood or reputation. In considering the potential effect on the defendant's reputation the court can be told of any prior convictions but magistrates who receive such information will not then be permitted to take part in a subsequent trial. In a gesture to the critics, there will be a right of appeal to the Crown Court against the decision that the trial be heard summarily. This will add to cost and delay but I imagine the Home Office calculate that it will not be used by many defendants.

One criticism made is that it will lead to two classes of justice—one for the defendant with prior convictions, the other for those who have none. The Royal Commission's view was that the presence or absence of prior convictions is a legitimate issue when it comes to consideration of the appropriateness of jury trial as a means for protecting someone's reputation. A person with prior convictions, at least if they are for similar offences to the current charge, has less of a reputation and to that extent—though only to that extent—has less of a claim for jury trial than someone who has no record. (Nine out of 10 of those who elect jury trial after the magistrates have said they could try the case have previous convictions.)

There is also opposition to the proposal on the ground that it will impact especially on the ethnic minorities because, it is said, they disproportionately distrust trial in the magistrates' courts. But in the absence of any evidence that magistrates are disproportionately likely to convict ethnic minority as compared to white defendants, I personally do not find the ethnic minority's alleged lack of confidence in the system sufficient reason for rejecting this reform. (The empirical evidence to date shows that both in Crown Courts and in magistrates' courts black defendants are actually more likely to be acquitted than white defendants.[29])

A great deal more will be heard of these arguments in the coming weeks.[30] Whilst the row rages in England it is worth

---

[29] For a survey of the evidence see David J. Smith, "Ethnic Origins, Crime, and Criminal Justice" in *The Oxford Handbook of Criminology*, (Maguire, Morgan and Reiner ed. 2nd ed., Clarendon, Oxford, 1997), pp. 704, 742–745. See also now B. Mhlangha, *Race and Crown Prosecution Service Decisions* (HMSO, October 1999), pp.18–19, a study of 6,000 cases in 22 CPS areas involving defendants under 22.

[30] For a powerful statement of the case against the proposal see for instance, V. Chapman, "Either way: the wrong way?", *Legal Action* (July 1999), p. 6. See also D. Wolchover and A. Heaton-Armstrong, "New Labour's attack on trial by jury", *New Law Journal* (October 30, 1998), p. 1613.

noting that in Scotland the defendant does not have a choice of court. The matter is decided there by the prosecutor which seems to give rise to no problem whatsoever.

It is safe to predict that jury trial will continue to be the mode of trial for contested cases in the Crown Court. The only doubt I see is over long fraud cases, a subject that has been under discussion now for some 30 years. One should of course do whatever can sensibly be done to improve the presentation of evidence for the jury in complex cases. It may also be that there are regulatory alternatives to criminal trials in some less serious cases, as tentatively recommended by the Runciman Commission.[31] If there is a criminal trial, I prefer that it be with a normal jury. I am not aware of any evidence that an ordinary jury cannot cope.[32] Moreover, I have yet to see an acceptable proposal as to what might replace it.[33]

In 1988, I opposed the abolition of the right of peremptory challenge (challenge without giving any reasons) of three potential jurors per defendant.[34] The Government alleged that the right was being abused by defence lawyers to eliminate from the jury anyone who looked educated. The evidence was entirely anecdotal and a Home Office study showed that use of peremptory challenges had no measurable impact on the conviction rate.[35] It seems to me that peremptory challenge was an acceptable and indeed desirable safety valve, giving the defendant a feeling of participation in the selection of the particular peers who are to try him. However it is now gone and I see little prospect that it will be restored.[36]

Certain categories of persons are ineligible for jury service because of their involvement in the justice business or disqualified by reason of their previous conviction, or exempt

---

[31] *op. cit.*, n. 13 above, at pp. 115–116.

[32] The best statement of the argument is still Mr Walter Merricks' Dissent to the Roskill *Fraud Trials Committee Report* (1986).

[33] See, for instance, the alternatives canvassed in the Home Office Consultation Paper *Juries in Serious Fraud Trials* (February 1998).

[34] Criminal Justice Act 1988, s. 118.

[35] J. Vennard and D. Riley, "The Use of Peremptory Challenge and Stand By of Jurors and their Relationship to Final Outcome" [1988] Crim. L.R. 731.

[36] In the *Crown Court Study*, barristers and judges in a large sample of cases were asked whether they wished to see the right of peremptory challenge restored. A clear majority of judges (82 per cent) and a bare majority of prosecuting barristers (56 per cent) said "No". A bare majority of defending barristers (56 per cent) said "Yes" (M. Zander and P. Henderson, *The Crown Court Study*, Royal Commission on Criminal Justice (Research Study No. 19, 1993), s. 6.2.5.)

because they are deemed to have more important business elsewhere. Recent Home Office research based on a sample of 50,000 persons summoned for jury duty has shown for the first time how few of those summoned for jury service actually serve. 13 per cent were ineligible, disqualified or excused as of right. (There is a strong case for drastically paring down these categories of exclusion so that more or less everyone is liable for jury duty, as is increasingly the case in the United States.) No less than 38 per cent of the sample were excused, typically on medical grounds or because of care of young children or elderly relatives or because they said they could not afford time off work. 15 per cent just failed to attend—in half those cases because the summons never reached them. That left 34 per cent. Of those, half had their jury duty deferred, usually because of work or holiday commitments and many later got a further deferral or were excused.[37] Next year the task of handling selection and summoning of juries is to be taken away from local courts and given to a new national clearing house in London. Maybe that will lead to tightening up the system.

The Home Office study may appear to support the widely held belief that jurors are not representative of the whole population, but the biggest study to date of the composition of the jury, carried out in 1993, suggested otherwise. Based on returns from a random national sample of over 7,500 jurors it showed that the socio-economic composition of English juries was remarkably close to the make-up of the general population.[38]

The Runciman Royal Commission was persuaded by the Commission for Racial Equality that in racially sensitive cases the judge should have the power to authorise a special procedure to achieve that the jury contain up to three members of the ethnic minority community. The jury bailiff would be instructed to draw names randomly until three such people were drawn. Lord Taylor, the then Lord Chief Justice, opposed the recommendation. In a speech to the Leeds Race Issues Advisory Council he said:

> "Though put forward for the best of motives, this proposal seems to me the thin edge of a particularly insidious wedge. The jury is the

---

[37] J. Airs and A. Shaw, "Jury Excusal and Deferral", (Home Office Research Findings, No. 102, November 1999).
[38] *Crown Court Study, op. cit.*, n. 36 above, ss. 8.13.3–8.13.6. The study was based on returns from 7,694 jurors in 757 trials—a response rate of 85 per cent.

foundation of our system. It is drawn at random from the law-abiding inhabitants of the locality in which a case is tried. We must on no account introduce measures which allow the state to start nibbling away at the principle of random selection of jurors".

Jurors must not be seen, he said, as "representing the views of the community, or of discrete parts of it, nor indeed of representing either the complainant or the victim".[39] On reflection, I think that on this issue Lord Taylor was right and the Royal Commission wrong.

I have always been a strong supporter of the jury system as incomparably the best known way of dealing with serious cases. Sometimes, admittedly, the jury gives a truly perverse verdict—one not only contrary to the evidence and the law but which is inexplicable even in terms of what is sometimes called jury equity. However, such cases seem to be very rare. Research suggests that generally the jury's verdict is explicable in light of the evidence,[40] and when it is not it usually seems to represent the jury reaction to what it considers to be an unjust law, an unfair prosecution or the threat of an excessive penalty. The jury's capacity to do justice in defiance of the law, as in the case of Clive Ponting, has been part of its historic role over the centuries[41] and we would be poorer without it.

There is as yet no right of appeal by the prosecution against a jury acquittal save in the rare situation where it can be established that the acquittal was probably the result of intimidation or other form of jury nobbling for which someone has been convicted.[42] Recently, however, the Law Commission has proposed, in the aftermath of the Stephen Lawrence case, that in certain circumstances a second trial should be allowed. The offence would have to be punishable with three or more years of imprisonment; the new evidence would have to strengthen

---

[39] *The Times*, July 1, 1995.
[40] See J. Vennard, "The Outcome of Contested Trials" in *Managing Criminal Justice* (D. Moxon ed., 1985), pp. 126–151; and "Evidence and Outcome: A Comparison of Contested Trials in Magistrates' Courts and the Crown Court", Home Office Research and Planning Unit, *Research Bulletin* (No. 20, 1986), p. 48.
[41] For research that traces that role see T.A. Green, *Verdict According to Conscience: Perspectives on the English Criminal Trial, 1200–1800* (Chicago University Press, 1985).
[42] This exception was introduced by the Criminal Procedure and Investigations Act 1996, s. 54.

the prosecution's case sufficiently to make it probable that a jury would convict; and the prosecution would have to show that the new evidence could not with due diligence have been obtained before the first trial. The decision would be for a High Court judge, subject to a right of appeal to the Court of Appeal. The court would have to be persuaded that a second trial was in the interest of justice.[43]

Despite the safeguards and restrictions, I am unhappy about the proposal. If a High Court judge allowed a second trial on the basis that a conviction was probable, in what sense could the defendant get a fair second trial?

Roughly one in four of those convicted by a jury appeals against conviction.[44] In the absence of any fresh evidence, the Court of Appeal, however, is understandably reluctant to overturn the jury's decision. It has not seen the witnesses or heard the evidence. Mastering the transcript of a trial sufficiently well to reach the conclusion that the jury got it wrong is a formidable task, especially in a lengthy case.[45] But occasionally it is prepared to make that judgment. In 1968, in the case of *Cooper*,[46] the court went so far as to say that it would quash the conviction if it had a "lurking doubt". ("[T]he court must in the end ask itself a subjective question, whether we are content to let the matter stand as it is, or whether there is not some lurking doubt in our minds which makes us wonder whether an injustice has been done. This is a reaction which may not be based strictly on the evidence as such; it is a reaction which can be produced by the general feel of the case as the court experiences it.") It would be remarkable if the Court actually applied that very liberal

[43] Law Commission, *Double Jeopardy* (Consultation Paper No. 156, 1999).
[44] In 1998, the Court of Appeal Criminal Division received 2,099 applications for leave to appeal against conviction. In the same year there were 9,562 defendants convicted after pleading not guilty to all counts. See *Judicial Statistics*, Cm. 4371, (1998), Tables 1.7 and 6.9. The comparable figures in 1997 were 2,318 and 10,152. (*ibid.*, Cm. 3980, (1997), Tables 1.7 and 6.9).
[45] Justice Michael Kirby, a distinguished Australian judge, has said that appeal judges typically do not have the time to consider the evidence properly. They may not even have time to read the whole of the transcript. ("They visit the evidence, on the invitation of counsel, skipping from one passage to another. Rarely do they capture the subtle atmosphere of the trial . . . These are the reasons why so much deference is paid to the advantages of the trial judge or jury, who see the evidence unfold in sequence and observe the witnesses giving their testimony." (*Miscarriages of Justice*, the Child & Co Lecture (London, 1991), p. 26.)
[46] [1969] 1 Q.B. 267.

approach and in practice it did not do so.[47] In fact, one of the court's most experienced past members, Sir Frederick Lawton in his evidence to the Runciman Royal Commission, said that the reason the judges did not apply the lurking doubt test was that they did not accept that "it was a sound way of administering criminal justice".

The Runciman Commission said that it understood the court's reluctance to quash a jury's verdict. However, it urged that "where on reading the transcript and hearing argument the Court of Appeal has a serious doubt about the verdict, it should exercise its power to quash".[48] That, it thought, would not undermine the system of jury trial.

Previously the Court had the power to quash a verdict if it was "unsafe or unsatisfactory".[49] The revised formula in the 1995 Criminal Appeal Act, s. 2, now provides for the verdict to be quashed if it is found to be "unsafe". There is no doubt that the single word "unsafe" still allows the court to quash the verdict on the ground that the jury got it wrong. But is the court supposed to apply the lurking doubt test?

In moving the Second Reading of the Criminal Appeal Bill, the Home Secretary said of s.2 that "in substance it restates the existing practice of the Court of Appeal".[50] During the Parliamentary debates on the Bill, Lord Taylor, the Lord Chief Justice, assured the House of Lords that the word "unsafe" would not result in any narrowing of the grounds of appeal.[51] Since "the lurking doubt" test was in bad odour with the judges and was honoured in the breach more than in the observance, this assurance was perhaps not worth much. Personally, I agree with Sir Frederick Lawton that the lurking doubt test is too broad. In my view the Court should apply the test proposed by the Royal Commission—it should quash the conviction where it has *serious* doubts about the jury's decision.

But the change from the old formula of "unsafe and unsatisfactory" to the new formula of "unsafe" raises a further

---

[47] For the research by K. Malleson establishing the facts see her "Miscarriages of Justice and the Accessibility of the Court of Appeal", [1991] Crim. L.R. 330; and *Review of the Appeal Process*, Royal Commission on Criminal Justice, (Research Study No. 17, 1993), pp. 23–25.
[48] *op. cit.*, n. 13 above, at p. 171, para. 46.
[49] Criminal Appeal Act 1968, s. 2.
[50] *Hansard*, H.C. Vol. 256, col. 24 (March 6, 1995).
[51] *Hansard*, H.L. Vol. 564, col. 311 (May 15, 1995).

fundamental issue. Does the new formula still permit the court to quash the conviction where it finds nothing wrong with the jury's verdict on the evidence, but where its concern is with the way the prosecution has conducted itself? The police fabricate a confession or secure one by beating up the suspect but there is plenty of other perfectly sound evidence that the accused was guilty. In one sense the conviction is safe. No doubt has been raised that the defendant committed the offence. On the other hand, the prosecution have behaved in a scandalous fashion. Can the Court of Appeal quash the conviction on the ground that it is not safe. The majority of the Royal Commission took the line that if there is solid evidence of guilt, the conviction is safe regardless of whether the prosecution has behaved badly. So far the judges have disagreed on this important issue of principle.[52] There have been cases where it has said it could not intervene and others where it said it could. My own strong belief is that the Court of Appeal must be free to express its repugnance for especially objectionable conduct of the police or other prosecution agencies. It is not sufficient to say that prosecution misconduct can be handled separately by disciplinary action against those concerned, even if that occurred, which too often is not the case.

I therefore dissented from the view of my colleagues on the Royal Commission:

> "The more serious the case, the greater the need that the system upholds the values in the name of which it claims to act. If the behaviour of the prosecution agencies has deprived a guilty verdict of its moral legitimacy, the Court of Appeal must have a residual power to quash the verdict no matter how strong the evidence of guilt. The integrity of the criminal justice system is a higher objective than the conviction of any individual."[53]

I believe it would be a sad day for our system if that principle were abandoned.

On a happier note it is very satisfactory that the Government implemented the Royal Commission's unanimous recommendation that a new system be introduced to deal with claims of

---

[52] See *R. v. Chalkley and R. v. Jeffries* (1998) 2 Cr.App.R. 79; [1998] 2 All E.R. 155 compared with *R. v. Mullen* [1999] Crim. L.R. 306.
[53] *op. cit.*, n. 13 above, at p. 235. See to the same effect A. Clarke, "Safety or Supervision? The Unified Ground of Appeal and its Consequences in the Law of Abuse of Process and Exclusion of Evidence" [1999] Crim. L.R. 108–116.

Criminal Justice

miscarriages of justice after all appeals have been exhausted. The old system left this process in the hands of the Home Secretary. The new system established by the Criminal Appeal Act 1995 places it with the Criminal Cases Review Commission, an agency independent of government. The CCRC started work in January 1997. The general view seems to be that it has got off to a good start—though the backlog problem due to the volume of cases is a serious problem.[54]

Needless to say, the setting up of a better system for dealing with alleged miscarriages of justice does not affect the likelihood that a miscarriage of justice will occur. They occur for a great variety of reasons. Sometimes they are the result of wrongful acts by the police such as the fabrication or planting of evidence, perhaps the result of misplaced zeal to secure a conviction. Or they are the result of a failure by the prosecution to comply with the duty of disclosure of material that might assist the defence. This has now been officially acknowledged as so serious a worry that the new Director of Public Prosecutions has asked the CPS Inspectorate to inquire into it and the Home Office has set up an interdepartmental working party on the problem. The Attorney General is to issue new guidelines to prosecutors.[55] Often miscarriages of justice are the result of human failings, such as mistaken eye-witness evidence or other errors made by prosecution witnesses, including forensic scientists. Sometimes they are the result of a false confession by the defendant leading to a guilty plea, as happened in the case of Judith Ward. Quite often they are caused by the incompetence or inefficiency of the defence lawyers, in failing to get the defendant's case together or failing to pursue important lines of inquiry. Sometimes no one is really to blame. An innocent defendant has the bad luck to be convicted because of strong but misleading circumstantial evidence.

[54] The projected backlog in March 1999 represented a queuing time of between three and four years on the resources then available to the CCRC. Four out of five (79 per cent) cases were declared eligible to be considered. By November 1999 the Commission had taken a decision in 1,200 out of 2,826 cases. It was working on 468 cases and 1,158 were waiting to be dealt with. 68 cases had been referred back to the Court of Appeal. By November 1999 the Court had heard 25 of the 68 referrals. In 18, the verdict was quashed or the sentence was modified. In the other seven cases the conviction or sentence was upheld. (Information supplied by the CCRC, November 1999). In the seven years up to 1988 the Home Office referred 42 cases to the Court.
[55] Tom Sargant Memorial Lecture of the Attorney General, Lord Williams of Mostyn, November 29, 1999. (See www.justice.homepad.com.)

The system has a variety of procedures and rules in place to help reduce the risk that an innocent person will be convicted, though they provide protection equally to the guilty, which is right and proper since all suspects deserve certain basic rights. The content of these basic rights has been much debated over recent years.

A case in point is the "right to silence". The Runciman Royal Commission on Criminal Justice in 1993, like the Philips Royal Commission on Criminal Procedure in 1981, recommended by a majority that the traditional rule be preserved so that silence in the police station could not be made the subject of adverse comment by either the prosecution or the judge. But the Conservative Government in the person of Mr Michael Howard, the Home Secretary, rejected the view of the two Royal Commissions. If a suspect being questioned under caution fails to mention a fact that he later relies on at his trial, which it would have been reasonable to have expected him to mention at that time, the jury can now be invited to consider whether that failure is evidence of guilt.[56] The caution had to be changed to warn the suspect that exercising his right to silence might prejudice his case.[57] The changes were implemented by a Conservative Government but the then Labour Opposition, led by Mr Jack Straw as Shadow Home Secretary, did not strenuously object. I sense they are unlikely to be reversed by this or a future administration.

What difference have the changes made? Home Office research has shown that the proportion of suspects giving "no comment" interviews has fallen from 10 per cent to six per cent, a sizeable reduction.[58] (Not surprisingly, the reduction was greatest among those who had legal advice.) But it does not follow that this translates into more convictions or even more prosecutions. Earlier research on the outcome of over 1,000 interviews had shown that four-fifths (80 per cent) of those who

---

[56] Criminal Justice and Public Order Act 1994, s. 34. See also ss. 36 and 37.
[57] "You do not have to say anything. But it may harm your defence if you do not mention when questioned something which you later rely on in court. Anything you do say may be given in evidence." Research showed that only one in eight "ordinary people" understood the crucial second sentence. (*Counsel*, September–October 1995, p. 4.)
[58] T. Bucke and D. Brown, *In police custody: police powers and suspects' rights under the revised PACE codes of practice* (Home Office Research Study No. 174, 1997), p. 35.

were silent in the police station were convicted, often after pleading guilty. In the control group consisting of suspects who did answer questions, the proportion convicted, curiously, was slightly lower (77 per cent)![59] The researchers, one of whom was a senior police office, commented, "Abolishing the right to silence might reduce the irritation felt by the police, but would probably do little to increase the number of successful prosecutions". That was always my own assessment.

Some might say that if it makes little difference in practice, why all the fuss about the importance of the right to silence. For me "the fuss" was not only about the likely dangers especially to the innocent, but the point of principle that if the burden of proof lies on the prosecution, it is wrong to penalise the suspect for refusing to assist the police with their inquiries. (It is worth noting that a Parliamentary Committee in the State of Victoria, having come to this country to study Michael Howard's reform, recommended earlier this year that it not be copied there.[60])

Perhaps the most useful recently introduced safeguard for the suspect in the police station is tape-recording of interviews. The original object was both to discourage improper police questioning and to provide evidence of it when it occurs. The police, understandably, started very hostile but quickly came to see its value—having the suspect's confession on tape increases the proportion of guilty pleas. The tapes also reduce courtroom battles over what the suspect did or did not say. A side-benefit has been that the tapes provide valuable raw material both for research and for police training. It turns out from such research by Professor John Baldwin, that general ineptitude in questioning is statistically a much greater problem than unacceptable methods of questioning.[61] In a sample of 600 interviews,

---

[59] S. Moston, G. Stephenson, T. Williamson, "The Incidence, Antecedents and Consequences of the Use of the Right of Silence During Police Questioning", *Criminal Behaviour and Mental Health* (1993), p. 3.

[60] State of Victoria Scrutiny of Acts and Regulations Committee, *Inquiry into the Right of Silence* (March 1999).

[61] J. Baldwin, *Video Taping Police Interviews with Suspects—an Evaluation* (Police Research Series, No. 1, Home Office, 1992). A quarter of the 600 interviews were "not very well conducted" and 11 per cent were conducted "poorly". (Table 3, p. 14) Contrary to mythology, "four out of every five were with such co-operative or compliant individuals that they should have presented no serious difficulty to a moderately competent interviewer" (p. 18).

Unsurprisingly, it seems that the police *do* use unacceptable methods more

Baldwin thought that the officer's manner was "unduly abrasive or aggressive" in only four per cent.[62]

Access to legal advice for suspects is more problematic. The number who avail themselves of the possibility of free advice in the police station is large—in 1997–1998 some three-quarters of a million at a cost to the taxpayer of £100 million. The problem is, first, the 60 per cent or so of suspects who choose not to ask for it and the further five or so per cent who ask but for one or another reason do not get it. It seems reasonable to assume that at least some of these would have benefited from competent legal advice. But there is also a question about the quality of the help given by those who do get it. Research has shown that this is not by any means always good enough. The Legal Aid Board's latest report stated: "There are significant areas where all types of police station advisers have high levels of non-compliance with the standards of performance laid down by the Law Society."[63] This seems to be as true of solicitor advisers as of those who are not solicitors.[64]

The failings of defence lawyers have been documented in a devastating piece of research by Professor Michael McConville and colleagues at Warwick University. The main accusation of their book, *Standing Accused*,[65] is that defence lawyering is for the most part geared toward the routine production of guilty pleas.

> "Advisers of all grades fall in with police routines and are responsive to police expectations that the private interview with the client [in the police station] will be over in a matter of minutes."[66]

> often in very serious cases, at the risk that the evidence will be held to be inadmissible. See J. Pearse and G.H. Gudjonsson, "Measuring influential police interviewing tactics; a factor analytic approach", *Legal and Criminological Psychology*, (Vol. 4, 1999), pp. 221–238. In half of the 18 cases in the study the suspect pleaded guilty. In no fewer than six of the other nine, the case was dismissed because of irregularities concerning the conduct of police interviewing.

[62] Baldwin, *op.cit.*, n. 61 above, at p. 18.
[63] Legal Aid Board Annual Report (1997–1998), p. 37, para. 5.12.
[64] "Accredited representatives carry out their functions overall as well as solicitors (in some respects better and in some less well)" (*ibid.*). See generally L. Bridges *et al.*, *Improving Police Station Legal Advice: The Impact of the Accreditation Scheme for Police Station Legal Advisers* (Law Society Research Study 1998); L. Bridges and J. Hodgson, "Improving Custodial Legal Advice" [1995] Crim. L.R. 104.
[65] M. McConville *et al.*, *Standing Accused* (Clarendon, Oxford, 1994).
[66] *ibid.*, at p. 100.

"Defence-advisers, most of whom are non-qualified staff, are less concerned with establishing the circumstances relating to the alleged offence than with securing from the client a promise to plead guilty. Their dealings with the clients, based in personal relationships, operate on the principle that the client has done something and should plead." [67]

Legally aided clients were not generally encouraged to tell their stories. Insofar as the story did emerge, the client was taught that it was not worth recording, that it would not persuade any court and that it should be abandoned in the face of the police evidence. Clients' statements were routinely disregarded. "Conviction is achieved in the office of their own adviser through a process whose methodologies most nearly resemble those of the police themselves."[68]

In the magistrates' courts it was rare for the defendant to have a defence based on work done by his lawyers—"any success defence lawyers have at trials themselves tends to be a product of what they can achieve 'on their feet' in court and whatever 'turns up' on the day."[69]

In crown court cases there were a few firms that engaged in proactive defence lawyering—preparing the case well in advance, seeking out witnesses, sending inquiry agents to draw up plans of the scene of the crime, employing forensic experts— but such firms were "quite exceptional".

The Bar was not any better. A few barristers were strongly committed to cases and were careful to test the underlying basis of a guilty plea, but most barristers were not[70]:

"Strikingly on the hearing day at court, but also in conferences in chambers, barristers evince little interest in scrutinising the evidence or in attempting to convince the defendant of its weight and probative value. Rather, conferences are treated as 'disclosure interviews', the purpose of which is to extract a guilty plea from the client."[71]

It is also a regrettable fact that barristers in criminal cases tend to get their instructions very late. The *Crown Court Study* done

---

[67] *ibid.*, at p. 159.
[68] *ibid.*, at p. 160.
[69] *ibid.*, at p. 238.
[70] The differential rate of guilty plea rate amongst barristers had emerged in an earlier study by Professor M. McConville and Professor John Baldwin in *New Law Journal* (October 27, 1977), p. 1040.
[71] *op. cit.*, n. 65 above, at p. 268.

for the Runciman Commission in 1993 showed that nearly a third (31 per cent) of defence barristers in contested cases only got the brief on the day before the hearing or on the day itself.[72] In a high proportion of cases the brief had been returned by another barrister.[73] If we were the defendant and knew that ours was such a case, I suspect we would not be too happy. But all efforts to find a workable solution to the problem of the returned brief have so far failed.

Of course most defendants plead guilty—well over 90 per cent in the magistrates' court and some 70 per cent in the Crown Court. One hopes that the reason is that most defendants *are* in fact guilty and cannot see any advantage in putting the prosecution to its proof. No doubt the fact that a defendant who pleads guilty will normally be entitled to a reduction of up to about one third of his sentence is a contributory factor. The Runciman Commission acknowledged that the sentence discount may sometimes lead an innocent defendant to plead guilty. But I do not think that the Royal Commission received a single submission suggesting that the sentence discount should be abolished.[74] It serves the interests of the prosecution in helping to secure a conviction, of the defendant in getting him a lower sentence and of the taxpayer in saving the expense of a trial. Whether the victim of the crime is always content about the reduced sentence must be doubtful, but at least the victim is spared the ordeal of having to give evidence.

If the tendency of defence lawyers is too easily to accept the police version of the case, this tendency is likely to be aggravated by the present strong emphasis on trying to get defendants to plead guilty at the earliest possible moment and the fast track processing of cases with the nationwide introduction of what are known as the Narey reforms. Pilot studies of "early first hearings" for straightforward guilty pleas and "early administrative hearings" for other cases showed that significant gains in terms of earlier pleas and rapid disposal were being

---

[72] *op. cit.*, n. 36 above, at p. 30, s. 2.1.3.
[73] 59 per cent of prosecution barristers and 44 per cent of defence barristers said the brief had been returned. (*ibid.*, s. 2.1.6, p. 32.)
[74] See, however, A. Ashworth, "The Impact on Criminal Justice" in B. Markesinis ed., *The Impact of the Human Rights Bill on English Law* (Clarendon, Oxford, 1998) p. 141 and A. Ashworth, *The Criminal Process: An Evaluative Study* (2nd ed., Oxford University Press, 1998) pp. 286–292.

achieved.[75] However, the danger is that defendants will be rushed into premature decisions as to how to plead; that the case will be dealt with before the defence are ready; and that courts will send defendants to prison without waiting for reports. The danger of rushing applies to the prosecution as well.[76]

The Government is currently preparing to launch a new major inquiry into the business of the criminal courts "on the model of Lord Woolf's inquiry into civil justice".[77] In September the Court Service published a 75-page Consultation Paper entitled *Transforming the Crown Court*. Commending the report, Lord Irvine the Lord Chancellor said, "I intend that today's perception of a fragmented and incoherent system with frustration, wasted time and cancelled hearings will soon be as out of date as the quill pen."[78] The ideas canvassed in the Consultation Paper included more rigorous case preparation, active case management according to streaming of cases, time limits enforced by sanctions (including on-the-spot fines for lawyers), appropriate IT support and changes in court listing to ensure that the case goes forward on the date scheduled. The inquiry will include magistrates' courts as well as Crown Courts.[79] I referred to my criticisms of the Woolf reforms in my last lecture. I would be concerned if innovations in civil justice based on the concept of judicial case

---

[75] According to research in the pilot areas, the time taken to deal with offenders from charge to disposal was cut from 85 days to 30 days for adults and from 89 days to 38 days for youths. Guilty pleas at a first hearing rose from 30 per cent to 55 per cent. (Ernst and Young, *Reducing Delay in the Criminal Justice System: Evaluation of the Pilot Schemes* (Home Office, 1999). For a critique of the figures and of the Government's implementation of the Narey Report see L. Bridges, *Legal Action* (October 1999), p. 6.

[76] For an assessment of the dangers see for instance, L. Bridges and M. Jacobs, *Reducing Delay in the Criminal Justice System—the Views of Defence Lawyers* (LCD Research Series No. 4, March 1999).

[77] LCD Press Notice, No. 349/99 (November 9, 1999).

[78] LCD Press Notice, No. 259/99 (September 8, 1999).

[79] The Lord Chancellor announced on December 14, 1999 that the inquiry would be conducted by Lord Justice Auld (*The Times*, December 15, 1999; LCD Press Notice No. 386/1999). The terms of reference were to review "the practices and procedures of, and the rules of evidence applied by, the criminal courts at every level with a view to ensuring that they deliver justice fairly, by streamlining all their processes, increasing their efficiency and strengthening the effectiveness of their relationships with others across the whole of the criminal justice system and having regard to the interests of all parties including victims and witnesses, thereby promoting public confidence in the rule of law". The review would be working to a deadline of December 2000.

management were to be applied to criminal cases before they have been properly tested. Obviously there will not be time for the inquiry to undertake or to commission research, but one hopes that at least any recommendations are piloted before being implemented unlike with the Woolf reforms.

Another impending controversial development is the introduction of state salaried defence lawyers as part of the new Criminal Defence Service under the Access to Justice Act 1999. I agree with those who believe that this could result in lower quality defence work though, as has been said, the present average level is unfortunately already not as high as it should be. But everything will depend on the way in which the new public defender service is set up—including, of course, the level of its funding and even more its staffing and leadership and whether it can build up a reputation for independence and good quality work. There are examples of high quality public defender services in other jurisdictions. It can be done. It should be done. As to whether it *will* be done, time alone will tell. I have to say that I incline to the pessimistic rather than to the optimistic view.[80]

If the Crown Prosecution Service is any indication of the likely quality of work by state salaried defence lawyers the omens are worrying. The recent Glidewell Report on the CPS gave a gloomy assessment:

> "The CPS is not seen generally as providing an attractive career opportunity nor, overall, do CPS lawyers seem to be held in as high professional regard as they and we would wish . . . "[81]

and

> "Overall the CPS has not succeeded in attracting enough lawyers with the skills and weight of experience which it needs, both to do its job properly and to establish a reputation for excellence . . . "[82]

It would be most unfortunate if the new Criminal Defence Service were to acquire a similar reputation.

---

[80] For a helpful discussion of the issues in light of Canadian experience, see D. O'Brien and J. Epp, "Salaried Defenders and the Access to Justice Act 1999", M.L.R., May 2000 (forthcoming).
[81] *Review of the Crown Prosecution Service*, Cm. 3960 (1998), p. 176, para. 13.
[82] ibid., p. 177, para. 14.

There has of course been a much longer running battle over whether the CPS should be permitted to conduct cases in the Crown Court. On this I support the view advanced by the Bar and senior judges rather than that espoused by the solicitors' branch. My reason for opposing extended rights of audience for the CPS is not primarily worry about the quality of CPS advocacy, though that is certainly a concern. My opposition is mainly based on the fact that CPS lawyers are employees of an organisation which unavoidably has a bureaucratic agenda. The Lord Chancellor tried to meet the point by section 42 of the 1999 Act, which provides that the duty to the court takes precedence over any other duty. But that does not deal with the point since, regardless of his seniority and experience, no employee in an organisation like the CPS can escape the pressures to conform with what I have called the bureaucratic agenda. At present, if the CPS and the barrister for the prosecution disagree about the handling of a case, the independent barrister's voice is there to challenge the CPS approach. When the CPS starts to use its new right to conduct contested cases on its own, that will no longer exist—to the potential detriment, I believe, of the quality of justice.

Quality is one of the themes constantly mentioned by both Ministers and the Legal Aid Board in referring to the plans for legal services under the 1999 Access to Justice Act. A crucial selling point of the new system of public funding of legal services, it is claimed, is that only firms that can satisfy the required quality of work standards to obtain contracts from the Legal Services Commission will be permitted to do the work. The auditing of standards through franchising by the Legal Aid Board may have had some effect in raising standards of work at least of some firms. But the danger, as a new study puts it, is that the audit rather than the legal aid client assumes central importance and that "managerialist concerns colonise legal practice".[83] The Board becomes the real client and the main

---

[83] H. Sommerlad and David Wall, *Legally Aided Clients and their Solicitors: Quality Perspectives on Quality and Legal Aid* (Law Society Research Study No. 34, 1999), p. 42. For the details of the present franchise requirements see Legal Aid Board, *Legal Aid Franchise Quality Assurance Standard*. For plans for the Quality Mark to be introduced for funded providers both in the profit and the not-for-profit sectors see Legal Aid Board, *Community Legal Service Quality Mark*, (Consultation Paper, August 1999). See also Hilary Sommerlad, "Man-

focus is keeping one's franchise. The challenge for the new Legal Services Commission, shortly to replace the Legal Aid Board, is finding a way to balance the need, on the one hand, for fund holders to be efficient and accountable and, on the other, to promote an environment that permits them also to provide genuine, as opposed to merely paper, quality of service.

* * *

There are so many important current developments affecting criminal justice that it is difficult to keep abreast of them and even more difficult sometimes to be sure whether they are to be welcomed or deplored. It is clear that some of the reforms are driven primarily by the Treasury's voracious appetite for cost cutting. Where money is to be saved, justice is liable to be at risk. But the fact that money is to be saved or that other efficiency gains are in prospect does not in itself *prove* that the proposed reform should be opposed by right thinking citizens. The best interests of defendants, of lay witnesses, of victims of crime, of jurors may also be served by improvements in the operation of the system. Certainly no one who has worked in the criminal justice system could deny that there is room for improvement in that regard.

After due allowance has been made for the objective that the system should run efficiently and economically, an even greater concern is that it should be so organised as to reflect the right balance between the proper interests of the prosecution and the proper interests of the defence. Experience suggests that striving to achieve that right balance is a task that will always defeat us—whatever balance is achieved there will always be someone calling for it to be changed. So the work of adjusting the balance is never done.

---

agerialism and the legal profession: a new professional paradigm", *International Journal of the Legal Profession* (Vol. 2, Nos 2/3, 1995), pp. 159–187; and "The implementation of quality initiatives and the New Public Management in the legal aid Sector in England and Wales", *ibid.* (Vol. 6, No. 3, 1999), pp. 311–342. See also the special issue of the *International Journal of the Legal Profession* on Competence and Quality Issues in the Legal Profession, (Vol. 1, No. 2, 1994).

4. Human Rights

The Human Rights Act 1998 is due to come into force fully in October 2000.[1] I believe that it will prove to be one of the most significant changes in the history of our legal system. It seemed appropriate to devote the last of my Hamlyn lectures on the State of Justice to this subject.

The story began 25 years ago almost to the day. On December 4, 1974, Lord Justice Scarman (as he then was), the Hamlyn lecturer for that year, called for an entrenched Bill of Rights to protect fundamental and inviolable human rights. Means had to be found, Scarman said,

> "whereby (1) there is incorporated into English law a declaration of such rights; and (2) these rights are protected against all encroachments including the power of the state, even when that power is exerted by a representative legislative institution, such as Parliament . . .[2]"

I covered the Scarman Hamlyn Lecture in my capacity as Legal Correspondent of *The Guardian*. Realisation of its potential political importance came the next day when I saw that the lecture was the front-page lead story.[3] The subject became a talking point. Organisations and individuals took positions on the merits of the issue—"for" or "against" a Bill of Rights, entrenched or otherwise. The position from which I took part in the campaign[4] was "for"—subject to recognition that having a

---

[1] It is already in force under the devolution legislation for Scotland and Wales—the Scotland Act 1998 and the Government of Wales Act 1998. For details see, for instance, Lester and Pannick, eds., *Human Rights Law and Practice* (Butterworths, 1999) pp. 275–285, 313–314.
[2] *English Law—the New Dimension* (1974) at p. 18.
[3] December 5, 1974.
[4] See especially Michael Zander, *A Bill of Rights?* (1st ed.), Barry Rose, 1975 (4th ed., Sweet & Maxwell, 1997).

Bill of Rights is not a recipe for a quiet life. (What one might call two and a half cheers.)

The concrete issue from the outset and throughout was whether to incorporate the European Convention on Human Rights (the "ECHR"). In the 1970s, the call for a Bill of Rights in the form of the ECHR was supported by prominent individuals in both the Conservative and the Labour parties. The Liberals were in favour. In 1978, a House of Lords Select Committee, dividing six to five on non-party lines, recommended that the ECHR be incorporated into United Kingdom law—a recommendation that was confirmed in a debate in the House of Lords in November 1978.[5]

But for almost 20 years, from 1974 to 1993, both the Conservative Party and the Labour Party were united in rejecting the idea. The Conservatives had a variety of reasons for their opposition to the whole idea of a Bill of Rights. First, being conservative they were not favourable to a major constitutional innovation. It might be alright for newly emerging Commonwealth countries, on which Britain invariably conferred a Bill of Rights as part of the post-colonial heritage, but the mother country did not need it. Also, a Bill of Rights was likely to upset too many apple carts. These fears were expressed even by Lord Denning. A Bill of Rights with entrenched clauses, he said in 1976, would be "contrary to all our history and tradition".[6] It could be utilised by individuals who might "tend to disrupt and embarrass our society".[7] It might be "taken advantage of by disgruntled people who will bring proceedings before the courts challenging the orderly system of our country".[8] They might be turned down, but there would be a great deal of litigation: "people praying in aid of these fundamental rights, as they say, and giving much embarrassment and disturbance to society".[9] (It should be said that a decade later Lord Denning had changed his mind and supported incorporation of the ECHR.[10])

The Conservative distrust of the idea of a Bill of Rights also revolved around concern for the position and reputation of the

---

[5] For the blow-by-blow account of the history of the campaign to secure incorporation of the ECHR, see the writer's book, n. 4 above, Chap. 1.
[6] *Hansard*, H.L. Vol. 369, col. 797 (March 25, 1976).
[7] *ibid.*, col. 798.
[8] *ibid.*, col. 800.
[9] *ibid.*
[10] A. Lester, "Fundamental Rights: The United Kingdom Isolated?" [1984] P.L. 46 at 63, n. 83.

judges. This feeling was expressed by the distinguished Scottish judge Lord McCluskey in his 1987 Reith Lectures. Everyone agreed that the judges should stay out of politics but a Bill of Rights would inevitably drag the judges into politics:

> "Lawmaking should be left to lawmakers, policy making to responsible policy-makers. And that's just the problem with a constitutional Bill of Rights. It is inevitably a charter of enduring super-rights, rights written in delphic words but in indelible ink on an opaque surface. It turns judges into legislators . . . It makes the mistake of dressing up policy choices as if they were legal choices. It asks those whose job it is to know and apply the law to create and reform the law . . . If legislators don't tell us precisely what the words mean, then the words will mean what the judges say they mean."[11]

Also, he said, it would raise the whole question of the cast of mind of judicial appointees. This fear was expressed by Lord Mackay speaking as Lord Chancellor in 1996. If the ECHR were incorporated or a Bill of Rights enacted,

> "The question which would then be asked, and to which an answer could not be postponed indefinitely, is whether introduction of such a political element into the judicial function would require a change in the criteria for appointment of judges, making the political stance of each candidate a matter of importance as much as his or her ability to decide cases on their individual facts and the law applicable to those facts."[12]

Following on from that, he suggested, was the question whether the appointment of the judges should be subjected to political scrutiny of the sort familiar in the United States.

I have never discounted the weight and the reality of these concerns.[13]

The Labour Party's objection to a Bill of Rights also related primarily to the judges, but from a different perspective. One strain of the argument was that a Bill of Rights is too powerful a tool to be entrusted to judges and is incompatible with democratic principles. Difficult, controversial or important social and

---

[11] *Law, Justice and Democracy* (BBC, 1987), p. 34. See to like effect Lord McCluskey's speech on the Second Reading of the Bill—*Hansard*, H.L. Vol. 582, cols 1265–1269 (November 3, 1997).
[12] "Parliament and the Judges—A Constitutional Challenge", speech by Lord Mackay to the Citizenship Foundation, July 8, 1996.
[13] They are considered in my book, *op. cit.*, n. 4 above, at pp. 105–108, 146–151.

political issues should be decided by the elected legislature rather than by appointed judges. This position had no answer to the obvious historical fact that governments and legislatures cannot be relied on to protect civil liberties and human rights.

The Labour Party, like the trade unions, also traditionally held that the judges could not be trusted to get it right. They were drawn from a narrow social class, mainly educated at Oxbridge and then had a narrow professional formation at the Bar. They were members of the Establishment. Issues that come up under a Bill of Rights commonly involved unpopular minority groups. The judges tended to side with the big battalions against the little man or the ordinary citizen.[14] The chief exponent of this point of view was Professor John Griffith of the LSE Law Department, notably in his book *The Politics of the Judiciary*.[15]

The debate rumbled on in a desultory fashion in the 1970s, 1980s and into the 1990s. With the two main political parties opposed to incorporation it seemed clear that nothing would come of it. The turning point came on a particular day (March 1, 1993) when John Smith, speaking as leader of the Labour Party, committed himself to incorporation of the ECHR into our law. In his speech, given under the auspices of Charter 88, Smith said that he wanted to see "a fundamental shift in the balance of power between the citizen and the state—a shift away from an overpowering state to a citizen's democracy where people have rights and powers".[16]

> "The quickest and simplest way of achieving democratic and legal recognition of a substantial package of human rights would be by incorporating into British law the European Convention on Human Rights."[17]

The European Convention, he said, was a mature statement of rights which had been interpreted and applied over many years by an expert court. Our law had been subject to it since 1950. What was needed now was to make that protection "real and accessible to our citizens, instead of a last resort available after years of struggle and litigation". Technically an Act of Parliament could not be entrenched, but effective protection of the

---

[14] These issues are discussed in my book, *op. cit.*, n. 4 above, at pp. 77–93.
[15] (5th ed. Fontana, 1977.)
[16] "A Citizen's Democracy", delivered at Church House, Westminster, March 1, 1993.
[17] *ibid.*

Human Rights Act "from undermining by the courts" would be achieved by a clause requiring that any other Act that intended to introduce laws inconsistent with the Convention must do so specifically and in express terms—by what in the jargon is called "a notwithstanding clause"—a technique that had been used in the 1982 Canadian Charter of Rights and Freedoms.[18]

I do not know how it came about that Mr Smith made that speech. I suspect that his close friend and adviser Lord Irvine of Lairg may have had something to do with it. What is certain is that in 1993, Labour Party policy suddenly and unexpectedly shifted from "no" to "yes".[19] From then on the question was no longer whether but when and how.

The Human Rights Act 1998, for which the Lord Chancellor, Lord Irvine, deserves the main credit, is an intriguing piece of legislation.[20] Much praise (perhaps too much praise) has been heaped on the subtlety of its construction.[21] My own sense is that the admirers may have underestimated problems that lie in store because of the way the Act is structured.

In important respects the Act is very different from the model propounded in 1993 by John Smith. Smith assumed that the ECHR would be incorporated into United Kingdom law and that, even if technically not entrenched, Parliament would only be able to depart from the Convention if it did so expressly. Lord Irvine chose a different approach.

The relevant articles of the ECHR do not become part of United Kingdom law as such.[22] They are attached to the Act in a

---

[18] s. 33 of the Charter permits the legislature to derogate from a provision in the Charter providing it does so expressly: "Parliament . . . may expressly declare in an Act . . . that the Act or a provision thereof shall operate notwithstanding a provision included in section 2 or sections 7 to 15 of this Charter."

[19] See *A new agenda for democracy: Labour's proposals for constitutional reform* (September 1993).

[20] Much attention will no doubt be paid to what was said in the Parliamentary debates on the Bill. For a very helpful collection of the most important Ministerial statements see Francesca Klug, "The Human Rights Act 1998, *Pepper v. Hart* and All That", [1999] P.L. 246–273.

[21] On the Third Reading, Lord Lester of Herne Hill went so far as to describe it as "a jewel of a Bill" and "brilliantly conceived and exquisitely well executed"— *Hansard*, H.L. Vol. 585, cols 805, 835 (February 5, 1997).

[22] There was some confusion in the debates on the Bill as to whether this amounted to incorporation. Lord Irvine said both that it did and that it did not. (*Hansard*, H.L. Vol. 584, col. 1266 (January 19, 1998); Vol. 585, col. 421 (January 29, 1998), *ibid*., col. 850 (February 5, 1998). The Home Secretary said that it did—*Hansard*, H.C. Vol. 306, col. 771 (February 16, 1998).

Schedule, as the "Convention rights". The meaning of the Convention rights is to be found in the decisions over the past 40 or more years of the European Court of Human Rights and of the Commission. In the ECHR system, the final arbiter as to the meaning of the Convention is the Strasbourg court. Its decisions are binding on all Member States. Section 2 of the Human Rights Act states that in deciding any question regarding the Convention rights, the courts are required to take the decisions of the Strasbourg court into account.[23] The phrase "take into account" means, by definition, that they are not binding. If they are not binding they need not be followed.

However, the crucial section 6 of the Act provides first, that it is unlawful for a public authority to act in a way which is incompatible with a Convention right, and then that a "public authority" includes "a court or tribunal".

So it is unlawful for public authorities, including the courts, to act incompatibly with the Convention but at the same time the courts are not bound by any decision of the Strasbourg court and can therefore follow them or not as they think right. What does this apparent contradiction in terms mean? No satisfactory answer to that question is to be found either in the Act or in the Parliamentary debates—or indeed elsewhere. I fear that it will cause confusion.

The problem I am addressing will arise where there is a conflict between the interpretation of the Convention that emerges from the Strasbourg jurisprudence on a point currently before an English judge and what the judge thinks English case law on that point ought to be. If, say, the judge concludes that Strasbourg law on the point is X and that X sits well with current English case law, he will of course declare X to be the rule of English law. To say that this is because section 6 requires him to do so is untrue. The section 6 point is only tested if the court sees a conflict between Strasbourg law and our common law. If the judge sees such conflict and prefers the Strasbourg interpretation to the English rule, he is free to pronounce the Strasbourg interpretation as the new rule of English law. It seems that this would be so even where the English rule flows

---

[23] s. 2(1) states that it must take into account any relevant judgment, decision, declaration or advisory opinion of the Court, any opinion or decision of the Commission or any decision of the Committee of Ministers.

from pre-1998 Act decisions by higher courts that would otherwise be binding.[24] So, a High Court judge or the Court of Appeal could apparently decline to follow a decision of the House of Lords! (For instance they might hold that the House of Lords' famous decision in *Rondel v. Worsley*[25] on the advocate's immunity from negligence liability is incompatible with Article 6 of the Convention in granting lawyers a blanket immunity, thereby denying the citizen access to a court.) It is extraordinary that this potentially dramatic effect of the Act on the doctrine of precedent was not raised in either House of Parliament during the debates on the Bill.

There is a further major problem concealed in the section 6 duty of courts not to act inconsistently with Convention rights. The Act basically gives remedies for acts done by public authorities. (Introducing the Bill on the Second Reading the Lord Chancellor said, "We decided, first of all, that a provision of this kind should apply only to public authorities, however defined and not to private individuals. That reflects the arrangements for taking cases to the convention institutions in Strasbourg. The convention has its origins in a desire to protect people from the misuse of power by the state, rather than from the actions of private individuals."[26]) But what if the litigation is between private litigants? Are the courts required by section 6 to apply Strasbourg law to the case and if not, why not? But, if so, does this not mean that the interpretation of the Convention emerging from the Strasbourg jurisprudence has been given far greater impact and reach than has been generally appreciated? Virtually no attention was given to this important question during the Parliamentary debates (though the Lord Chancellor, speaking during the Committee Stage of the Bill, said, "We also believe that it is right as a matter of principle for the courts to have the duty of acting compatibly with the convention not only in cases involving other public authorities, but also in developing the common law in deciding cases between individuals. Why should they not?"[27]). This question of the so-called horizontal effect of the Act has already provoked a considerable

---

[24] See Lord Cooke of Thorndon, "Mechanisms for Entrenchment and Protection of a Bill of Rghts: The New Zealand Experience" [1997] EHRLR 490 at 493.
[25] [1969] A.C. 191.
[26] *Hansard*, H.L. Vol. 582, cols 1231–1232 (November 3, 1997).
[27] *Hansard*, H.L. Vol. 583, col. 783 (November 24, 1997).

volume of learned writing.[28] The better view seems to be that although there is no new general requirement to ensure compatibility of private common law with Convention rights, the courts will be under a duty to consider Strasbourg jurisprudence as an indication of principles to be taken into account. A private party will not be able to initiate proceedings against another solely on the basis of a Convention right, but the Convention will nevertheless have what Sir Stephen Sedley has called a cascade effect[29]—carrying a flow of rights and remedies from the Convention through the Act and into the courts, and from the courts into enforceable forms of recourse to the Convention rights—for instance of privacy. (Dealing with the question whether the Act gave the courts the green light to develop the law of privacy the Lord Chancellor said: " . . . the courts will be able to adapt and develop the common law by relying on existing domestic principles in the laws of trespass, nuisance, copyright, confidence and the like, to fashion a common law right to privacy".[30])

I believe that the Convention and its jurisprudence will provide much nourishment for the development of the common law, but that when the courts regard the Strasbourg material as unhelpful or unwise, they will respond unpredictably. Sometimes they will feel constrained by the obligation in section 6 of the Act not to act inconsistently with a Convention right; sometimes, remembering that they are not bound by Strasbourg decisions, they will decline to follow them. (Dealing with a Conservative amendment that would have made Strasbourg decisions binding on English courts, Lord Browne-Wilkinson said: "I have found the jurisprudence of the European Court of Human Rights excellent, but a major change is taking place. We are now seeing a wider range of judges adjudicating such matters, a number of them drawn from jurisdictions 10 years ago not famous for their observance of human rights. It might be dangerous to tie ourselves to that".[31]) Again there was

---

[28] See for instance, G. Phillipson, "The Human Rights Act, 'Horizontal Effect' and the Common Law: A Bang or a Whimper?", *Modern Law Review* (1999, Vol. 62), pp. 824–49 and the references cited in n. 1 of that article. Phillipson suggests (at p. 825) that "The Act's impact on the common law governing relations between private persons is prima facie its area of greatest obscurity".
[29] Sir Stephen Sedley, *Freedom, Law and Justice*, (Sweet & Maxwell, 1999), p. 31.
[30] *Hansard*, H.L. Vol. 583, col. 785 (November 24, 1997).
[31] *Hansard*, H.L. Vol. 583, col. 513 (November 18, 1997). There are 41 States that have ratified the ECHR. The 17 that ratified since 1992 are all Eastern European countries.

virtually no discussion of the problem in the debates on the Bill in either House—though during the Committee stage the Lord Chancellor did say, "The Bill would of course permit U.K. courts to depart from existing Strasbourg decisions and upon occasion it might well be appropriate to do so and it is possible they might give a successful lead to Strasbourg".[32]

I wonder whether it will prove to have been wise to have laid on the courts the duty not to act incompatibly with the Convention rights. (The Canadian courts are not subject to the equivalent requirement *vis-à-vis* the Charter of Rights and Freedoms.)

When a conflict between Strasbourg law and English law arises in the form of an English statute, the Human Rights Act *does* give the judges a specific direction. For Leslie Scarman in his 1974 Hamlyn lectures, control of an aberrant legislature was the main reason to have a Bill of Rights. John Smith, in his 1993 lecture, equally argued that the courts should be able to rule legislation to be contrary to the ECHR unless Parliament specifically negatived that intention. But the 1998 Act rejects that approach. On the contrary, in a case of a clear conflict between a Strasbourg rule and one that derives from an English statute, it is the statute not the Strasbourg rule that prevails. As Ministers were at pains to make clear, Parliamentary sovereignty reigns supreme. The same is true where the conflict is between a Strasbourg rule and an English rule in delegated legislation that flows directly and inevitably from a statute. The judges have to follow the English rule in the statutory instrument in defiance of Strasbourg law.

The Act (section 4) provides that if that situation arises in the High Court or above, the judges can issue "a declaration of incompatibility". The effect of such a declaration is to pass the ball to the Government by inviting use of the procedure for fast track legislation to eliminate the inconsistency between Strasbourg law and English law. The fast track procedure allows the Minister to introduce a statutory instrument (called "a remedial order" under section 10) to override the previous offending statute or statutory instrument. Statutory instruments that override primary legislation are known in the business as "Henry VIII clauses"—a pejorative description signifying that they are unpopular with those who have a concern for constitutional principles and the operation of the normal democratic

---

[32] *Hansard*, H.L. Vol. 583, col. 514 (November 18, 1997).

process. A "Henry VIII clause" is something close to overriding legislation by Ministerial decree. It is true that governments control the legislature almost completely and can force through virtually any primary legislation, but Ministerial power exercised through a "Henry VIII clause" by way of delegated legislation is even more dramatic.

When considering the democratic deficit involved in remedial orders under the Act, it is worth noting that such an order can contain "such incidental, supplemental, consequential or transitional provision as the person making it considers appropriate"[33]; it can be retrospective in its effect[34]; and it can amend primary legislation other than that which contains the incompatible legislation.[35] It is a very far-reaching power.[36]

Such an amending statutory instrument normally[37] requires an affirmative resolution in both Houses of Parliament, but that is saying very little. Governments have no difficulty in getting such an affirmative resolution. The Act provides for a special procedure for fast track "remedial orders"[38] the main ingredient of which is that the order has to be laid before parliament for a longer than usual period of time, so giving more time for opposition to build up. But since the government can normally force anything through, this extra time is unlikely to be of much consequence.

A court's declaration of incompatibility creates no duty on the Government to act by way of fast-track remedial action. The Act says that the fast track procedure can be activated where the Minister "considers that there are compelling reasons"[39]—a formula that slightly tips the balance against action. There have to be not merely reasons but "compelling reasons".

---

[33] Human Rights Act 1998, Sched. 2, para. 1(1)(a).
[34] *ibid.*, para. 1(1)(b). But no one can be found guilty of an offence solely as the result of the retrospective effect (*ibid.*, para. 1(4)).
[35] *ibid.*, para. 1(2)(a).
[36] The European Communities Act 1972, s. 2(2) permits a statutory instrument to give effect to a Directive by amending an Act of Parliament. For commentary on the Henry VIII clause aspects of the 1998 Act see, for instance, D. Feldman, "The Human Rights Act 1998 and constitutional principles", [1999] L.S. 165 at 187–191.
[37] In cases of urgency this requirement is waived but the remedial order lapses after 120 days unless it has been approved by Parliament. (Schedule 2, para. 4.)
[38] Schedule 2.
[39] s. 10(1)(b).

In the Parliamentary debates on the Bill, Ministers gave the impression that governments would be quick to use the fast track procedure in order to eliminate the embarrassment of an inconsistency between Strasbourg law and English law. (The Lord Chancellor, for instance, said on the Bill's Second Reading, "If a Minister's prior assessment of compatibility is subsequently found by declaration of incompatibility to have been mistaken, it is hard to see how a Minister could withhold remedial action".[40]) If that were so, I would be concerned. I prefer that the kind of problem likely to be in issue be dealt with by ordinary, proper legislation rather than by what is virtually a Ministerial decree.

Contrary to what Ministers proclaimed, my own prediction is that governments will tend to be very reluctant to use the procedure. First, there is the normal problem of getting government to do anything. Secondly, governments are especially slow in responding to civil liberties concerns which so often affect unpopular causes. It is foolish to expect governments to have their interests at heart. Thirdly, government, rightly or wrongly, will often prefer the English rule or practice to the Strasbourg rule with which it has been declared to be inconsistent. It would be odd if in that situation it did not simply sit tight and wait for the complainant to take the case to Strasbourg by way of appeal. (The Home Secretary said that if the courts decided that the abortion law was incompatible with the Convention the government "could say we were very sorry but we disagreed . . . Then the party to the proceedings . . . [could] exercise her right of appeal and go to Strasbourg".[41])

So why is it said that the Human Rights Act constitutes a major advance in terms of protection of civil liberties and human rights? We have had access to the ECHR for more than 30 years since December 1965, when Britain first accepted the right of individual petition to Strasbourg. Use of this right of individual petition started slowly but it has now become something of a flood. In the 38 years from 1960 to 1998, there were over 6,000 cases brought against the United Kingdom that reached the stage of being registered cases,[42] an average of some

---

[40] *Hansard*, H.L. Vol. 582, col. 1229 (November 3, 1997).
[41] *Hansard*, H.C. Vol. 317, cols 1301, 1303 (October 21, 1998).
[42] In 1997, of 12,469 provisional files opened by the Commission, only 4,750 applications (38 per cent) were registered.

160 per year. In 1998 alone there were 300. Some experts predict that the Human Rights Act will have the effect of reducing the number of cases going to Strasbourg. I do not take that view. On the contrary, I believe it is likely to increase them.

The Strasbourg system can provide a remedy. In that same period to 1998, there were 52 cases against the United Kingdom in which the Strasbourg Court found one or more violation of the Convention (as against 35 in which no violation was found). Findings of violations do sooner or later result in action to put the matter right by the respondent government.

So the Strasbourg system works. In what way then is access to the ECHR different because of the 1998 Act? One reason is that it is quicker and easier to bring a case as a complainant in the United Kingdom courts than in Strasbourg. Cases in Strasbourg take an average of five years to reach a decision—though now a case that ends in Strasbourg will take even longer because it will first have to go through the British system. Access will be easier physically in that Strasbourg is geographically quite a distance. However, more importantly, it will be easier psychologically. Most solicitors have never taken a case to Strasbourg and have no idea how to do so (it simply would not occur to them), whereas taking a case in an English court is something solicitors know about.

Moreover, the 1998 Act permits a person to take his Convention points not simply in proceedings that he has initiated, but in a case being brought against him, for instance, in criminal proceedings. The experts all predict that the bulk of Human Rights Act points will be taken by defendants in criminal cases. It is obviously much easier to take Convention points in an existing action one is defending than initiating a case oneself.

Another reason why the Act changes everything is because of the enormous increase in knowledge about the ECHR. Partly this is through formal training. So, for instance, all the 3,000 full and part-time judges are attending a one-day training seminar run by the Judicial Studies Board. There will be training for the 30,000 lay magistrates and the clerks who advise them. (A sum of £4.5 million was allocated to this official training.)

There are numerous training courses for private practitioners. (The role played by lawyers in deciding what cases to bring and what Convention points to argue will be of great importance. If too many ill-conceived actions are brought or far-fetched Convention points are taken by advocates, there is a danger that the judges will become hostile.[43])

There has already been an outpouring of books on the subject. Legal journals are full of articles about the implications of the Act for a great variety of substantive fields of law. University law schools will be stimulated to devote even more attention to the ECHR than before and more students will take the relevant optional subject.

Civil servants and other officials will become more sensitised to the ECHR dimension in their work. The Act provides (section 19) that a Minister must state before the Second Reading of any Bill that in his view its provisions are compatible with the Convention rights, or that the Government is putting the Bill forward even though it does not consider it compatible with the Convention. Every new Bill, therefore, now has to be Convention proofed.[44] But the effect on civil servants will be much more far-reaching than this. Any act by a civil servant that impacts on citizens is an act by a public authority that could come under scrutiny through legal proceedings in any court. So every such action or decision should equally be Convention proofed.

In November 1998, every Government Department was asked to send to the Human Rights Unit in the Home Office an initial assessment of the likely impact of the Act on their work, with further progress reports at six-monthly intervals. They were asked to indicate any factors that might affect the date of implementation of the Act—which, incidentally, is why implementation was postponed until October 2000. The minutes of the second meeting of the Government inter-departmental Task Force on the Human Rights Act stated that "Convention rights

---

[43] Sir Stephen Sedley put the same point in his 1998 Hamlyn Lectures:

"If Convention rights are used simply as fallbacks where other arguments have failed, the Human Rights Act may well become devalued . . . If on the other hand, lawyers . . . learn to discern the viable human rights issues in fact situations and to argue these with discrimination and skill as organic elements of their case, the courts themselves will be helped to understand the relevance and purpose of the Human Rights Act and a human rights culture may begin to take root." (*op.cit.*, n. 29 above, p. 21.)

[44] s. 19. Lord Hoffman has written of s. 19, "Speaking for myself, I would take such a statement extremely seriously and would be very reluctant to decide that such a measure was not in fact compatible." ("Human Rights and the House of Lords", *Modern Law Review* (Vol. 62, 1999), pp. 159, 162.)

need to be considered in every aspect of current systems and procedures".[45] The Lord Chancellor's Department, for instance, has a Project Board to oversee the work of implementation, chaired by a senior LCD official and, interestingly, including judicial representation in the persons of Lord Justice Brooke and Lord Justice Sedley. Departments have drawn up plans for training programmes both in terms of general awareness for all staff and more detailed training for staff with a particular interest such as Bill teams. In some cases (including that of the Crown Prosecution Service) training is to be on the basis of detailed internal guidance material. Departments have been encouraged to pin-point issues on which challenges under the ECHR are more likely—and legislation and other appropriate action is already being brought forward to deal with some of these issues pre-emptively.[46]

(Some of these initiatives, it has to be said, are not particularly welcome. The new rule that cases in the small claims court must be heard in public, a response to the Article 6 requirement that in the determination of his civil rights everyone is entitled to a public hearing, risks making such hearings less welcoming to the ordinary citizen. The same requirement may play havoc with some of the major ombudsman systems in allowing parties to demand an oral hearing where previously the ombudsman would have dealt with the complaint perfectly satisfactorily much more speedily and cheaply by himself. One can imagine banks and insurance companies, for instance, claiming a right to an oral hearing to the great disadvantage of the complainant. It seems that that is a price one has to be prepared to pay.)

All this activity on so many fronts and at so many levels is producing a huge increase in knowledge about the ECHR which will translate into far greater impact of the Convention. Lawyers who never thought of taking a case to Strasbourg are already gearing up to use the Act. The trickle-down effect will gradually extend wider and wider—to newspapers and the media generally, to politicians and other opinion formers, to universities and schools and to an extent to the general public. In 1978, summarising the arguments for a Bill of Rights, the House of Lords

---

[45] Minutes of the Second Meeting of the Interdepartmental Task Force (March 9, 1999), para. 4.1.
[46] For further details see Amanda Finlay, "The Human Rights Act: The Lord Chancellor's Department's Preparations for Implementation" [1999] E.H.R.L.R. 512–518.

Select Committee said that the ECHR "seems likely to have a far more practical effect on legislators, administrators, the executive, citizens as well as legislators, if it ceases to be only an international treaty obligation and becomes an integral part of the United Kingdom law".[47] That is now happening. The ECHR, which hitherto has made only a slight impact on the general consciousness, will gradually become a familiar presence in our body politic.

However, the success or failure of the whole enterprise depends on the judges, and not just the senior judges, for Convention points can be taken in any court and any tribunal. How will they respond? Will the judiciary be politicised? Will changes have to be made in the way the judges are selected?

The attitude of the most senior judges toward the Convention is today broadly positive. There was a time when the judges greeted arguments put to them based on the ECHR almost with disdain. But gradually this changed, largely as a result of the educative effects of the advocacy of a small number of practising barristers amongst whom Anthony Lester Q.C. (now Lord Lester of Herne Hill) deserves special mention.[48] By the mid-1990s, almost all the Law Lords, both serving and retired, had been won over to the idea of incorporating the ECHR into United Kingdom law and several of them were active in promoting that cause.[49] In the 21 years between 1975 and 1996, the ECHR was cited in 316 judgments—of which 60 per cent occurred in the five years from 1991.[50]

Until now the impact of the ECHR has been restricted. In his maiden speech in the House of Lords in 1996, Lord Bingham of Cornhill, then the newly appointed Lord Chief Justice, outlined a number of ways in which the ECHR was of relevance.[51] In particular, where a United Kingdom statute was ambiguous, the

---

[47] *Report of the Select Committee on a Bill of Rights* (House of Lords paper 176, June 1978), p. 32.
[48] Lord Lester also played a pre-eminent role on the subject in the House of Lords, as was rightly acknowledged in generous tributes paid to him in the last stages of the Third Reading of the Human Rights Bill. See *Hansard*, H.L. Vol. 585, cols 837, 838, 839–840 (Februrary 5, 1997).
[49] See Lord Lester, "The Mouse that Roared: the Human Rights Bill 1995" [1995] P.L. 198, n. 1.
[50] F. Klug and K. Starmer, "Incorporation through the back door?" [1997] *Public Law*, pp. 223, 224. For a survey see Murray Hunt, *Using Human Rights Law in English Courts* (Hart Publishing, 1997).
[51] *Hansard*, H.L. Vol. 573, cols 1465–1467 (July 3, 1996).

courts would presume that Parliament intended to legislate in conformity with the Convention; and where the common law was uncertain, unclear or incomplete, the courts would rule so as to be in conformity with the Convention. There were limits however. As the decision of the House of Lords in *R. v. Home Secretary, ex p. Brind*[52] made clear, the courts could not use the ECHR to construe an unambiguous statutory provision, nor could the ECHR be a direct source of rights and obligations.

Section 3(1) of the Human Rights Act changes the position by instructing the judges that *"so far as it is possible to do so*, primary legislation and subordinate legislation must be read and given effect in a way which is compatible with the Convention rights" (emphasis added). This instruction applies to past as well as future legislation which makes it practicable now not only to test past statutes but to reopen previously decided cases. The effect may be considerable.[53] As Lord Cooke of Thorndon has said, section 3(1) "will require a very different approach to interpretation from that to which the United Kingdom courts are accustomed. Traditionally, the search has been for the true meaning; now it will be for a *possible* meaning that would prevent the making of a declaration of incompatibility."[54] (Emphasis added.) The Lord Chancellor has said that "the courts will be required to interpret legislation so as to uphold Convention rights unless the legislation itself is so clearly incompatible with the Convention that it is impossible to do so."[55] Lord Lester believes that means that courts should prefer a strained but possible meaning over an interpretation "that more closely reflects the structure and text of the impugned

---

[52] [1991] 1 A.C. 696.

[53] For discussion and references to relevant statements during the passage of the Bill, see Lester and Pannick (ed.), *Human Rights Law and Practice* (Butterworths, 1999), pp. 23–24, 72–73.

[54] *Hansard*, H.L. Vol. 582, col. 1272, (November 3, 1997).

[55] Lord Irvine of Lairg, "The Development of Human Rights in Britain" [1998] P.L. 221 at 228. He cited E.U. decisions. ("In cases involving European Community law, decisions of our courts already show that interpretative techniques may be used to make the domestic legislation comply with the Community law, even where this requires straining the meaning of words or reading in words which are not there". (*ibid.*)). On the Second Reading of the Bill, Lord Irvine said that s. 3(1) would ensure that in choosing between two interpretations of a statute, one compatible and the other incompatible with the ECHR, "the courts will always choose the interpretation which is compatible. In practice this will prove a strong form of incorporation." (*Hansard*, H.L. Vol. 582, cols 1230–1231 (November 3, 1997.))

legislative provision".[56] If that is right[57]—and it may be[58]—I would regard it as unfortunate.[59]

Whether it is technically right or not, I imagine that many judges will in practice resist that view. I think they will especially be slow to adopt a strained though possible interpretation of legislation which the Parliamentary debates indicate clearly was not what Parliament intended. I believe that there is a serious risk of bringing discredit on the entire enterprise if the judges are thought to be required to twist words used in legislation in order to achieve the objective of compatibility with the ECHR. This is of course particularly so where the Strasbourg rule seems to the judges to be less enlightened or sensible than our own.

I also believe that English judges will often prefer the English to the Strasbourg solution by applying, by analogy, the equivalent of what in Strasbourg-speak is called "the margin of appreciation" allowed to each national system. Some have suggested that the margin of appreciation has no application internally since it is a device used by an international tribunal to define the reach of the international standard within the national system. But I believe that the English courts will, rightly, want to give a certain weight to decisions and acts of the legislature or of the executive, to prevailing practice and procedure and to judicial precedent. There will be a measure of judicious deference to decisions duly arrived at by the relevant authorities.[60]

[56] Lord Lester, "The Art of the Possible" [1998] E.H.R.L.R. 665 at 669.
[57] In the view of Mr Francis Bennion, the legislative history of the provision shows so much "vagueness and confusion in the minds of the Act's promoters" as to render it "largely useless, because it is inconsistent and one can 'prove' almost anything by it". ("Section 3(1) of the Human Rights Act 1998" [1999] J.P. 984–985.
[58] Attempts to replace the word "possible" with "reasonable" failed in both Houses of Parliament—*Hansard*, H.L. Vol. 583, col. 535 (November 18, 1997); *Hansard*, H.C. Vol. 313, cols 421–422 (June 3, 1998).
[59] Section 3(1) is very similar to s. 6(1) of the New Zealand Bill of Rights Act 1990 which states: "Wherever an enactment can be given a meaning that is consistent with the rights and freedoms contained in this Bill of Rights, that meaning shall be preferred to any other meaning". Lord Cooke of Thorndon has said this formula does not authorise a strained interpretation (*Ministry of Transport v. Noort* [1992] 3 N.Z.L.R. 260 at 272). See also Lord Cooke, "The British Embracement of Human Rights" [1999] E.H.R.L.R. 243 at 250.
[60] See, for instance, D. Pannick, "Principles of Interpretation of Convention Rights under the Human Rights Act and the Discretionary Area of Judgment" [1998] P.L. 545; Helen Fenwick, "The Right to Protest, the Human Rights Act and the Margin of Appreciation" (1999) 62 M.L.R. 491–514.

The Supreme Court of Canada, in the context of the Canadian Charter of Rights and Freedoms, said that there are cases in:

> "the social, economic and political spheres where the legislature [or other authorised person] must reconcile competing interests in choosing one policy among several that might be acceptable."[61]

In those circumstances,

> "the courts must accord great deference to the legislature's choice because it is in the best position to make such a choice ... [T]he courts are not specialists in the realm of policy-making, nor should they be. This is a role properly assigned to the elected representatives of the people ..."[62]

The Strasbourg Court has said that the extent to which the margin of appreciation operates varies according to the context,[63] and the United Kingdom courts will need to develop a sense for the appropriate scope for deference to decision-making in areas of policy of the executive, the legislature and other organs and institutions. The judges will not be thanked for needlessly destabilising existing systems that were working perfectly well. A case in point was the recent startling decision of the Scottish appeal court retrospectively invalidating the appointment of all the 120 or so temporary part-time undersheriffs who handled 25 per cent of all the work in the sheriff courts.[64] The court struck down the system of probationary appointments, thereby creating serious disruption to the administration of justice despite the fact that there was no evidence

---

[61] *Libman v. A.G. of Quebec* (1983) 3 B.H.R.C. 269 at 289, para. 59.
[62] *ibid.*, at para. 60.
[63] See for instance *Buckley v. United Kingdom* (1996) 23 E.H.R.R. 101.
[64] *Starrs v. Procurator Fiscal, Linlithgow, The Times*, November 17, 1999. Undersheriffs, who handle 25 per cent of the work of sheriff courts, are appointed by the Lord Advocate, who is also in charge of the prosecution system. Appointments are from year to year and can be terminated without any set procedure. The Scottish Court of Criminal Appeal held that a judge who has no security of tenure and whose appointment was subject to annual renewal was not "independent" within the meaning of Art. 6 of the ECHR. The decision has menacing implications for many forms of part-time or temporary judicial appointment which are used extensively in the U.K. system. The Lord Chancellor may, for instance, withdraw an Assistant Recorder's authorisation to sit "at any time if he considers this to be in the public interest". (LCD, *Judicial Appointments*, March 1999, p. 19.)

and indeed no suggestion that it worked improperly.[65] This decision has serious implications for many valued forms of temporary or probationary appointments including Assistant Recorders. Such surprising decisions will sorely test the resolve of supporters of the Human Rights Act.

It was always inevitable that some of the judicial decisions given under the Act would be highly controversial and that they might provoke discussion not only of the merits of the particular case but of the credentials of the judges themselves to make such decisions. We have already seen the beginnings of this development in the fall-out from "l'affaire Hoffmann" in the Pinochet saga, resulting from Lord Hoffmann's most unfortunate failure to make public his connection with an arm of Amnesty International, which was an intervenor in the case.[66]

The call for further reforms in the system for appointing judges will probably gain in strength.[67] It cannot be denied that a judge's approach to policy issues may influence his judicial decisions.[68] It equally cannot be denied that a Bill of Rights significantly increases the overall policy quotient in judicial decision-making. It is therefore not surprising that having a Bill of Rights focuses attention on the system for appointing judges.

There are two main issues. One is whether the composition of the bench is sufficiently inclusive. That is an issue of importance

---

[65] "His Lordship did not doubt that the system had been operated by successive Lords Advocate with integrity and sound judgment, free from political considerations, and with careful regard to the need to respect judicial independence . . . His Lordship wished to make it plain that he was not suggesting that any temporary sheriff had ever allowed his judicial conduct to be influenced by any consideration of how he might best advance his prospects of obtaining the renewal of his appointment or his promotion to a permanent appointment." (per Lord Reed, *The Times*, op. cit., n. 63 above, p. 29).

[66] For the House of Lords decision overturning its own earlier decision because of Lord Hoffmann's failure, see *R. v. Bow Street Metropolitan Magistrates, ex p. Pinochet Ugarte (Amnesty Internationl intervening) (No. 3)* [1999] 2 All E.R. 97. For the Court of Appeal's guidelines on when a judge should step down, see *Locabail (U.K.) Ltd v. Bayfield*, *The Times*, November 19, 1999.

[67] The best contemporary discussion of the relevant issues is Kate Malleson, *The New Judiciary: the effects of expansion and activism* (Ashgate, 1999), Chap. 4.

[68] For a recent study based on that proposition see David Robertson, *Judicial Discretion in the House of Lords* (Clarendon, Oxford, 1998). Basing himself on a statistical analysis of decisions by 15 Law Lords in the period 1985–1995, Robertson demonstrates that it was predictable which way a case would be decided by reference simply to what judges—and especially what combination of judges—was sitting. (See further M. Zander, "Who judges matters", *New Law Journal*, January 8, 1999, p. 5.)

whether or not one has a Bill of Rights, but a Bill of Rights perhaps gives it extra point. I do not share the view, recently expressed by the Law Society, that, subject to the requirement of appropriate individual quality, "the judiciary as a whole should reflect the whole of society".[69] But there is much to be said for the proposition that the judiciary should be *more* representative of society—even if it would make no difference to actual decisions—because its present composition, overwhelmingly white, male, educated at public school and Oxbridge,[70] is so often the source of critical comment.

Certainly, at the very least, the system should not discriminate against qualified persons—which raises in particular the question of discrimination in regard to gender and race. The fact that the number of women and persons of ethnic background on the bench is still woefully small[71] is not, I think, the result of direct discrimination. The Lord Chancellor's Department in recent years has increasingly been looking for suitable persons to appoint.[72] The reason has much more to do with the insufficient numbers of qualified candidates at that level of seniority which should improve as more women and non-white practitioners move into that age bracket. This hope is supported by the statistics. Applicants for Assistant Recorder on average have 20 years' seniority. Women barristers of more than 20 years Call are 12 per cent of the practising Bar but 18 per cent of Assistant

---

[69] Law Society's Submission to Sir Leonard Peach's Enquiry into appointment of judges, September 28, 1999. By contrast, the LCD's evidence to the Home Affairs Select Committee stated: "The Lord Chancellor has no plans to reconstitute the professional judiciary to reflect the composition of society as whole". (*Judicial Appointments Procedures*, Session 1995–1996, Third Report, H.C. 52-1, Vol. II, para. 2.3.3.)

[70] The proportion who went to Oxbridge is currently around 80 per cent—see Malleson, *op. cit.*, n. 67 above, p. 104.

[71] The figures do not look good. In 1999, of the 149 judges of High Court or above, only nine (six per cent) were women. Of the 558 Circuit judges, 36 (six per cent) were women. Less than one per cent of Circuit judges were from an ethnic minority background. (Figures about the ethnic background of judges have been collected only since 1991.)

[72] Details of some of the efforts made recently are given in the first annual report on *Judicial Appointments, 1998–1999*, Lord Chancellor's Department, Cm. 4449, pp. 6–7, 15. For instance, to support the principle of equal opportunity, there is now recognition of the effect of career breaks for child rearing, the upper age limit for appointment can be lifted, sitting as Assistant Recorder can be in blocks rather than spread over several years.

Recorders.[73] Barristers from ethnic minorities with more than 20 years' are four per cent of the bar and 3 per cent of Assistant Recorders.[74] There may be an additional problem of reluctance, for a variety of reasons, of some qualified persons to apply[75]—which may or may not be something that can be altered by exhortation and encouragement.[76]

There are relatively few former solicitors on the bench.[77] The main reason is that it has been thought that the necessary background, at least for sitting in the Crown Court or the High Court, is substantial experience as an advocate in the higher courts, experience that most solicitors do not have. Responding to the publication of Sir Leonard Peach's inquiry on judicial appointments,[78] the Lord Chancellor said that there may in the past have been too great a tendency to promote the best advocates from the Bar to the bench with insufficient attention to the possibility of promoting other lawyers working in the courts: "The skills and experience needed to be a judge may perfectly well be shown by a successful litigation solicitor as by a leading advocate, and indeed that has already been proved to be the case by the appointment of solicitors to the bench."[79] This was a clear signal that Lord Irvine will be looking for more senior solicitors to appoint, at least if they have significant

---

[73] *Judicial Appointments, op. cit.*, n. 72, p. 8, para. 1.16. Dr K. Malleson has drawn the LCD's attention to the fact that these figures are misleading in that they understate the proportion of women in the relevant cohort. This is because the LCD's figures include older barristers of over 30 years' Call when there were very few women. Taking the cohort of between 15 and 30 years' Call, the proportion of women at the Bar (18 per cent) was almost identical to that of female Assistant Recorders (17 per cent).

[74] *ibid.*

[75] Since 1994 judicial posts have been advertised and in 1997 this was extended to the High Court. Of the seven High Court judges appointed in 1998–1999, four had applied and three had been invited to accept appointment. (*Judicial Appointments, op. cit.*, n. 72 above, p. 23.)

[76] Dr Kate Malleson, of the London School of Economics Law Department, has been commissioned by the LCD to undertake research to help identify the reasons why those who are currently underrepresented on the bench, especially women and members of the ethnic minorities, might be disinclined to apply for appointment.

[77] In 1999, of 149 judges of the level of High Court and above, only one was a former solicitor. Former solicitors were 13 per cent of the Circuit judges and 10 per cent of Recorders.

[78] Sir Leonard Peach, *An Independent Scrutiny of the Appointment Processes of Judges and Queen's Counsel in England and Wales*, December 1999.

[79] LCD, Press Notice, No. 379/1999, December 3, 1999.

litigation experience. However, it would be surprising if this led to a dramatic increase in the number of solicitor appointments, so one can anticipate a continuation of the Law Society's current strident complaints.

Now that judicial appointments are advertised, it is important that ways be found to encourage qualified persons on both sides of the profession to apply for judicial posts.[80] It is no less important that ways be found to increase the number of persons from non-traditional backgrounds to enter the legal profession so as to broaden the pool from which appointments are made. But these policies are easier to state than to implement in such a way that they make a difference. If they do not prove successful, and I suspect they may not, it is difficult to think of an effective way forward. (I share the virtually universal opposition to any form of affirmative action or positive discrimination programme to make the bench more representative.) These problems will undoubtedly continue to plague us.

There is also the question whether the system for appointing judges should continue to include the traditional soundings taken from senior members of the bench and the profession or whether it should be supplanted or at least supplemented by some form of Judicial Appointments Commission. To some, the system of what have been called "secret soundings"[81] is reprehensible. The Law Society's evidence to Sir Leonard Peach's Inquiry went so far as to suggest that it should be scrapped.[82] But Sir Leonard's conclusion was that to abandon the consultation process "would be a neglect of a valuable input into the assessment", though he made some suggestions for improving the process including an opportunity for the applicant to nominate up to six consultees who would automatically be contacted.[83]

---

[80] Sir Leonard Peach's Report (*op. cit.*, n. 78 above) includes in Appendix F the 42 recommendations by a Joint Working Party on Equal Opportunities in Judicial Appointments and Silk set up by the Lord Chancellor.
[81] Applicants now receive a Guide for Applicants which sets out, *inter alia*, the identities of those who will be consulted.
[82] See *Law Society's Gazette*, September 29, 1999, p. 1.
[83] Other proposals included asking applicants to state their own views on their suitability and re-design of the consultation form to ensure that comments are related to the requirements of the post as opposed to general comments. Consultees should also be asked to indicate the source of information they provide and if the source included others, whether they agreed or disagreed.

As currently operated,[84] the "taking of soundings" is a highly structured, major undertaking. (During a recent competition for Assistant Recorder, some 5,000 comments were received from nearly 1,900 people regarding 800 applicants.[85]) It may be that with the current numbers[86] the system has become too burdensome, but if it can be continued I would strongly support it in principle.[87]

Sir Leonard Peach recommended that a Commission for Judicial Appointments be established to provide an independent oversight or audit of the appointments system.[88] That recommendation was immediately accepted by the Lord Chancellor,[89] but the role of the new Commission would be limited to oversight of the existing system in an Ombudsman role. That is obviously desirable but is unlikely to satisfy those who argue for a more powerful Judicial Appointments Commission[90]— whether simply to advise on nominations coming from the executive or itself to be part of, or conceivably even be, the screening and nomination process.[91] The House of Commons

---

[84] For a description, see *Judicial Appointments, Annual Report, 1998–1999*, LCD pp. 10–11.

[85] *ibid.*, p. 11.

[86] In the 1970s the number of judicial appointments annually was 60–80. Today it is over 600.

[87] That was also the view of the House of Commons, Home Affairs Select Committee in its 1996 Report on *Judicial Appointment Procedures* ("The consultation system may be a good method of building an informed picture of candidates' qualities.") (Session 1995–1996, 52–I, para. 62). It thought that "the value of a consultations network might be diminished if a Judicial Appointments Commission were to play a part in selecting judges" (*ibid.*, para. 142).

[88] *op. cit.*, n. 78, pp. 24–27.

[89] LCD Press Notice, No. 379/1999 (December 3, 1999).

[90] See JUSTICE, *The Judiciary in England and Wales* (1992). In 1995, the Labour Party adopted the proposal for a judicial appointments commission in its policy document *Access to Justice*. Shortly after the May 1997 General Election, Lord Irvine announced that he would be consulting on the merits of the proposal, but a few months later in October 1997 he stated that because of the pressure of the LCD's workload he had decided to shelve the matter for the time being. (LCD Press Release, October 9, 1997.) In 1998, William Hague, leader of the Conservative Party, was reported to have said that it was considering parliamentary confirmation hearings for judges (*The Times*, February 25, 1998).

[91] For discussion of different models see a report commissioned by the LCD in 1997: Dr C. Thomas and Dr K. Malleson, *Judicial Appointments Commissions: The European and North American Experience and the Possible Implications for the United Kingdom*, LCD Research Series, No. 6/97; and Malleson, *op. cit.*, n. 67, pp. 125–152.

Home Affairs Committee concluded unanimously, "we have not been persuaded that the quality of appointees would necessarily improve if a Judicial Appointments Commission were to be established."[92] I tend to agree with that view, though the appointment of such a Commission could help to diminish any public concern about the composition of the judiciary. For the moment, however, I count myself amongst those who say they are not convinced of the need for such an innovation.

The other quite separate question, which relates more directly to the introduction of a Bill of Rights, is whether the views of judges should be explored and taken into account before they are appointed, and, if so, how that should be done. Interviews for those applying for judicial office at the lower levels are now the rule.[93] But such interviews, which are of the order of 45 minutes, do not explore the candidate's views on social policy questions.[94] Should that be part of the process? Should such interviews be introduced for candidates for higher judicial office and, if so, should they be held in public? I imagine that most English lawyers and judges would recoil from such an idea. I confess that I recoil from it myself. In some common law countries, interviews with prospective judges at the highest level have been introduced and seem to be working. The judges appointed to the Constitutional Court in South Africa, for instance, are required to attend a public interview before the Judicial Services Commission. Dr Kate Malleson reports that "despite the initial misgivings which were expressed by lawyers and judges in South Africa about the use of such interviews, the general opinion now seems to be strongly supportive of their use as a means of identifying the broad approach of the candidates to the judicial role".[95] Sir Sydney Kentridge Q.C. has described the process as follows:

---

[92] *op. cit.*, n. 87 at para. 142.
[93] All those appointed to the post of District Judge, Assistant Recorder, Recorder and Circuit Judges are interviewed by a panel consisting of a judge, someone from the LCD and a lay person.
[94] The purpose of the interview is to test the candidate in regard to the criteria for appointment. These are under three headings: Legal Knowledge and Experience; Skills and Abilities; and Personal Qualities. Personal Qualities are said to be Integrity; Fairness; Understanding of people and society— sensitivity to different ethnic and cultural backgrounds; Maturity and sound temperament; Courtesy and humanity; and Commitment (Guidance Notes for Consultees, November 1999).
[95] Malleson, *op. cit.*, n. 67 above, p. 100.

"Many of the questions put to the judicial candidates were searching and some of them were personal. But the proceedings were nothing like the more exuberant proceedings in the Judiciary Committee of the United States Senate. I cannot say that any of the candidates enjoyed the experience but there is no reason to think that anyone has been put off high judicial office by the minor ordeal of the interview."[96]

If the interview is in private, I do not think it appropriate for the interviewing panel to explore the candidates' views on policy issues. The questioning process would risk being haphazard and subjective with each panel adopting its own approach. Moreover, since the main purpose is to satisfy a perception that the public needs to know the views of those who sit, especially those who sit in the higher tier of the judiciary, that need would not be met by private hearings. On the other hand, I find the idea of public hearings distasteful, demeaning both to the individuals being interviewed and to the judiciary as an institution. Perhaps that feeling is old fashioned. In any event, I doubt whether such questioning as might take place would in practice be sufficiently searching to be very revealing of, for instance, extreme racist, sexist or homophobic views. If it were very searching, attempting to explore attitudes in depth, it would, I think, be offensive—and anyway probably beyond the capabilities of those doing the interviewing.

In my view, candidates who are otherwise qualified for appointment to the judiciary should be rejected on the ground that their views on social policy issues are deemed to be unacceptable only in extreme cases, which in practice are very unlikely ever to occur. If that is right, there is no sufficient reason to try to explore their views. I do not believe that the process of trying to establish the facts in regard to a candidate's views is worth both the effort involved and the intrusiveness of the process. In other words, I am not persuaded that the objective of such public hearings is desirable and even if it were desirable, I do not think that the means to achieve it would be either effective or appropriate. Moreover, in the case of candidates for higher judicial office they have normally been on the

---

[96] S. Kentridge, "Bills of Rights—The South African Experiment", (1996) L.Q.R. 237 at 253.

bench for a considerable period so that, if it be important, their views can be studied through their judicial decisions.

* * *

The European Convention on Human Rights is a Bill of Rights couched in open-textured, broadly-phrased general principles,[97] qualified in many instances by other broad phrases.[98] It is the open-textured broad nature of the phrases that gives the citizen with a grievance more powerful access to a remedy by providing a peg for his argument. The courts have to measure existing systems, procedures and rules against the broadly stated fundamental principles—pro and con. Inevitably many of the cases brought or points taken under the Convention will be hopeless non-runners. But if an interference with a Convention right is once established, it is important in practical terms that the complainant has the advantage in that the burden of justifying the interference lies on the defending public authority. Cases are often won or lost depending on who has the burden of proof. The defending public authority has to show that the interference is prescribed by law, serves a legitimate purpose and is necessary in a democratic society. In order to satisfy the last test it has to show that the limitation serves a pressing social need and that it is proportionate.

If the burden of proof tips the balance toward the complainant, there is a different factor which for some judges might properly point the other way. That is the fact that whereas the citizen who loses in the United Kingdom courts on a Convention point can appeal to Strasbourg, the Government cannot.[99] If

---

[97] The right to life; the right not to be tortured or subjected to inhuman or degrading treatment; the right to liberty and security of person; the right to a fair and public hearing; the right to respect for one's private life and family life, etc.

[98] Thus, for instance, interference with the right to private life, family life, home and correspondence (Art. 8) is justifiable if it is "in accordance with the law and is necessary in a democratic society in the interests of national security, public safety or the economic well-being of the country, for the prevention of disorder or crime, for the protection of health or morals, or for the protection of the rights and freedoms of others".

[99] Art. 34 of the Convention as amended by Protocol 11, provides, "The Court may receive applications from any person, non-governmental organisation or group of individuals claiming to be the victim of a violation by one of the High Contracting Parties . . ."

it loses a case, its only recourse is the unattractive option of legislating to override the judicial decision, thereby presumably provoking a challenge in Strasbourg.

It will be some years before one can feel confident that the United Kingdom Bill of Rights represented by the Human Rights Act is permanent. The Conservative Party opposed the Bill. If in the early years there are too many decisions that provoke wrath or ridicule, it is, I suppose, conceivable that a future Conservative administration might scrap the whole experiment, but in my bones I feel that that will not happen.

In last year's Hamlyn lectures Sir Stephen Sedley said, "the moment of introduction of a human rights regime into the law of the United Kingdom, though millennial, is not arbitrary." It comes, he said, "at the end of a long trek by a handful of far-sighted campaigners led by Lord Scarman",[1] led, I would say, by Lord Scarman and Anthony Lester. I am proud to be able to say that I was one of those who 25 years ago joined that trek. I do not think that we were far-sighted, but we recognised a new possibility for our legal system equivalent to a paradigm shift. That is now about to be realised.

Those who are speaking and writing about this great historical event today mainly seem to be celebrating it without any hint of reservation. I cannot say that I am quite in that position, but although I have worries about the inevitable darker side of consequences that will cause considerable problems, I believe that in the coming decades and indeed centuries this will prove to be an immensely important development out of which much good will come in terms of justice for citizens.

The burden of leadership falls on the Court of Appeal and the House of Lords. We are fortunate indeed in the high calibre of these two courts at this crucial time. Lord Cooke of Thorndon has said that what is required of the judges will be a blend of "generosity, sensitivity to the spirit of the Convention and the legislation, and realism."[2] It will also require great wisdom.

---

[1] *op. cit.*, n. 29, p. 37.
[2] Lord Cooke of Thorndon, "The British Embracement of Human Rights", [1999] E.H.R.L.R. 242 at 259.

INDEX

ADR, 36–38
Access to Justice Act 1999, 7, 16, 74
Acquittal rate, 4, 53, 58
Airs, J., 61n
Allen & Overy, 36
Alternative Dispute Resolution, 35–38
Appeals by prosecution, 62
Ashworth, Andrew, 6n, 71n
Attlee Government, 7
Auld Inquiry, 72n

Baker & McKenzie, 36
Baldwin, Professor John, 34–35, 45, 68–69, 70n
Bingham, Lord, 91
"Birmingham Six" case, 3n
Bridges, Professor Lee, *et al*, 69n, 72n
Browne-Wilkinson, Lord, 84
Bucke, T., 67n
Brown, D., 67n

Cantley Committee, 27
Citizens' Advice Bureaux, 22, 23n, 31n
Clarke, A., 65n
Clifford Chance, 36
Collins, Professor Hugh, 29n, 38
Civil Justice Council, 39n
Civil Justice Review, 1985–88, 27
Community Legal Service, 9, 10, 18–23
Community Legal Service Partnerships, 10, 21
Conditional fee agreements, 15–18

Conservative Party against incorporation of ECHR, 78–79
Consumer Council, 34, 36
Contracted legal services, 13–14
Cooke, Lord, 83n, 92, 93n, 103
Court of Appeal attitude to jury verdicts, 64–65
Court fees, 39
Criminal Defence Service, 73
Criminal Cases Review Commission, 66
Criminal Justice (Mode of Trial) Bill, 57–60
Crown Court,
  costs of cases, 58
  justice in, 53–54
Crown Prosecution Service, rights of audience, 74
Crown Court Study, 1993, 60n, 61n, 70, 71n
Defence lawyers, 69–70, 71
Denning, Lord, 78
Diamond, Professor Shari, 56
Disclosure by the prosecution, 66
ECHR, *see* European Convention on Human Rights
Either-way offences, mode of trial, 57–60
Ernst & Young Report, 72n
European Convention on Human Rights (ECHR)
  delays, 88
  numbers of cases brought against U.K., 87–88
  right of individual petition, 87
Evershed Committee, 1953, 27
ex parte Brind, 92n
Felstiner, W., *et al*, 23n

Index

Fenwick, E., 93n
Finlay, Amanda, 90n
Franchised legal services, 74

Genn, Professor Hazel, 28n, 37n
  1999 study, 29–32, 33, 34
Glidewell Report, 1998, 73
Green, T.A., 62n
Green Form scheme ("legal help"), 13n, 18–19
Green Paper on legal aid, 1995, 7
Griffith, Professor J.A.G., 80
"Guildford Four" case, 3n
Guilty pleas, 71–72

Harris, D., et al, 28n
Hedderman, C., 58n
Henderson, P., 42n, 60n
"Henry VIII clause", 85–86
Hoffmann, Lord, 95
House of Commons Home Affairs Select Committee on Judicial Appointment, 99–100
House of Lords Select Committee on a Bill of Rights, 90–91
Howard, Michael, 67, 68
Human Rights Act 1998,
  "declaration of incompatibility", 85–86
  "horizontal effect", 83–84
  implementation, 77
  "remedial orders", 85–86
  statement of compatibility, 89
  s.2, 82n
  s.3, 92
  s.4, 85
  s.6, 82–84
  s.10, 85
  s.19, 89
Hunt, Murray, 91n

Illiteracy, proportion of population affected, 34n
Inquisitorial system, 52
Internet, 19
Irvine, see Lord Irvine

Jacob, Sir Jack, 44
James Committee, 1975, 53–54

Judges,
  appointment, 95–102
  attitude toward ECHR, 91–92
  background, 96
  ethnic minority, 96n, 97
  solicitor, 97
  women, 96–97
Judging a legal system, 2
Judicial Appointments Commission, 98–101
Juries,
  acquittal rate, 4, 58
  eligibility, 60–61
  long fraud cases, 60
  peremptory challenges, 60
  research, 54
  verdicts, 62

Kentridge, Sir Sydney, 100–101
KPMG Peat Marwick, 43–44
Kirby, Justice Michael, 63n
Klug, F., 81n, 91n

Labour Party,
  against incorporation of ECHR, 79–80
  for incorporation of ECHR, 80–81
Lawrence, Stephen, 62
Lawton, Sir Frederick, 64
Legal advice in police stations, 68–69
Legal aid,
  capping, 7, 8n, 10–11
  competitive tendering, 13–14
  contracted services, 13–14
  funding code, 14–16, 17n
  total cost, 7
  withdrawal, 8, 12
Legal Aid Act 1949, 7
Legal Aid Board Research Unit, 14, 15n
Legal Help (formerly Green Form scheme), 13n, 18–19
Lester, Lord, 71n, 78n, 81n, 91, 92–93, 103
Levi, Professor Michael, 42n
Lord Irvine of Lairg, 8, 14, 16, 24–25, 72, 81, 83, 84, 87, 92–93, 97
Lord Mackay of Clashfern, 7, 8, 39, 79n

Index

Mackay, *see* Lord Mackay
Magistrates,
  selection, 55
  stipendiaries, 56
  training, 54–55
Magistrates' courts,
  acquittal rate, 53–54
  costs of cases, 58n
  justice in, 53–56
  sentencing disparities, 55–56
  training of personnel, 55
Maguire case, 3
Malleson, Kate, Dr, 64n, 67n, 97n, 99n, 100
Mannheim, H., 55n
"Margin of appreciation", 93–95
McCluskey, Lord, 79
McConville, Professor Michael, 69–70
Mediation, 37–38
Merricks, Walter, 60
Middleton, Sir Peter, 8n
Montgomery, J.W., 54n
Moston, S., 68n
Moxon, D., 58n

Narey Review 1997, 71–72
Need for legal services, measurement of, 9–10

Oxford Socio-Legal Centre accident study, 28

Palmer, M., 36n
Pannick, D., 77n, 92n, 93n
Peach, Sir Leonard, 96n, 97, 98n
Peremptory challenge, 60
Philips Royal Commission on Criminal Procedure, *see* Royal Commission on Criminal Procedure
Phillipson, G., 28n
Pinochet case, 95
Pleasence, P., 14n, 15n
Police stations, legal advice in, 68–69
Ponting, Clive, 4, 62
Pottle, Pat, 4
Pre-action Protocols, 41
Prosecution appeals, 62
Prosecution disclosure, 66

Randall, Michael, 4
Rand Corporation study, 38, 42n
Rantzen, Esther, 24n
Returned briefs, 71
Right to silence, 67–68
Riley, D., 60
Roberts, Professor Simon, 36n
Robertson, David, 95n
Rosenberg, M., 42n
Roskill Committee, 1986, 60n
Royal Commission on Criminal Justice, 3, 6, 52, 57–59, 61, 64, 65–66, 67, 71
Royal Commission on Criminal Procedure, 67
Runciman Royal Commission on Criminal Justice, *see* Royal Commission on Criminal Justice

Scarman, Lord, 77, 85, 103
Scott, Sir Richard, 39
Seargant, J., 20n
Sedley, Sir Stephen, 84, 89n, 103
Sentence discount, 71
Settlement statistics, 28, 41
Shapland, J., 17n
Shaw, A., 61n
Small claims system, 34–35, 45
Smith, John, 80, 81, 85
Sommerlad, H., 74n
Starmer, K., 91n
Steele, J., 20n
Stephenson, G., 68n
Stipendiary magistrates, 56
Straw, Jack, 57
Supreme Court of Canada, 94
Susskind, R., 19n

Tape-recording of interviews, 68
Taylor, Lord, 61, 64
Thatcher, Mrs Margaret, 3
Thompson's, 48–49

Unmet need for legal services, measurement of, 9–10

Vennard, J., 60
Victoria, State of, right of silence, 68

Index

Wall, D., 74n
White Paper on legal aid, 1996, 8n, 11
Williamson, T., 68n
Winn Committee, 1968, 27

Woolf Report on Access to Justice, 27, 36, 39–49

Yarrow, S., 17n, 18n

Zander, Professor Michael, 38n, 40n, 65, 71, 77n, 78n, 79n, 80n, 95n